Next to GODLINESS

Finding *the* Sacred *in* Housekeeping

Edited by Alice Peck

Walking Together, Finding the Way®
SKYLIGHT PATHS®
PUBLISHING
Woodstock, Vermont

Next to Godliness:
Finding the Sacred in Housekeeping

2007 First Printing
Introduction and part opening text © 2007 by Alice Peck

See pp. 182–86 for a continuation of this copyright page.

Library of Congress Cataloging-in-Publication Data
Next to godliness : finding the sacred in housekeeping / edited by Alice Peck.
    p. cm.
  ISBN-13: 978-1-59473-214-0 (quality pbk.)
  ISBN-10: 1-59473-214-0 (quality pbk.)
  1. Home—Religious aspects. 2. Housekeeping—Miscellanea. 3. Cleaning—Miscellanea. I. Peck, Alice.

BL588.N49 2007
204'.32—dc22

                                                    2006035993

10 9 8 7 6 5 4 3 2 1
Manufactured in the United States of America

Cover design: Tim Holtz
Text illustrations: Melanie Robinson

SkyLight Paths is creating a place where people of different spiritual traditions come together for challenge and inspiration, a place where we can help each other understand the mystery that lies at the heart of our existence.

SkyLight Paths sees both believers and seekers as a community that increasingly transcends traditional boundaries of religion and denomination—people wanting to learn from each other, *walking together, finding the way.*

Walking Together, Finding the Way®
Published by SkyLight Paths Publishing
A Division of Longhill Partners, Inc.
Sunset Farm Offices, Route 4, P.O. Box 237
Woodstock, VT 05091
Tel: (802) 457-4000   Fax: (802) 457-4004
www.skylightpaths.com

This book is for Duane and Tyl.
You make my home.

CONTENTS

Contents

Contents

Contents

INTRODUCTION

Let the beauty we love be what we do.
There are hundreds of ways to kneel and kiss the ground.

—*Rumi*

I've always sought solace in cleaning: the repetition, the ritual of it, the opportunity to make where you are a better place, the bliss of just doing to *do*. During low points in my life, ironing pillowcases—a task that can be completed, and completed nearly perfectly—got me through rough patches. I remember helping my grandmother polish furniture when I was a child—I cleaned the table legs while she did the tops. Those times were always opportunities to ask "big" questions. When my husband and I packed up our apartment and cleaned the profound dust of the World Trade Center from our books and shook it from our pillows, we used this shared ritual as an opportunity to reflect and heal. Like my neighbor once said, "Cleaning house is my church."

At some point in everyone's life comes the time to clean up. It might be your kitchen after dinner; it might be your neighborhood after a disaster. One way or another, it must be done, and a considerable amount of time is spent doing it. Thinking about all these things led to the conception of *Next to Godliness*, a collage of writings that delves into the spiritual possibilities within the routine of housekeeping. This book does not give tips on cleaning; it is not a how-to guide for better homemaking. Instead, it offers insight into tasks that we all do, everyday, and attempts to uncover real beauty and divine truth amid our regular chores.

In *Next to Godliness* I have culled writings that explore the moments when giving in to the process of cleaning brings depth and meaning to our lives and reveals the sacred in the everyday. I have tried to do this by finding the places where a multitude of belief systems intersect—where clean and holy meet. The selections I've chosen are determinedly eclectic and ecumenical. I love finding dissimilar writers who reach the same conclusion by traveling different routes. For me, the best part of this search was discovering how strangers cross paths—the ways religions and voices you might never anticipate finding in the same volume intertwine and work together.

At first glance, you might question how the writers in this book are related; it is by pulling the common thread of the universal and straightforward process of cleaning, that the answer is revealed. Catholic nun Joan Chittister's interpretation of *The Rule of Benedict*, Tibetan Buddhist Chogyam Trungpa's explanation of external *drala*, and spiritual leader, educator, and social activist Booker T. Washington's discussion of how a minister's home reflects his preaching abilities all address the same topic: how the outside reveals the inside, the tangible reveals the abstract. Each contributor finds a similar answer through their different religious and historical perspectives. They all look at the same room through different windows.

When Louisa May Alcott cheerfully writes of making home in *Little Women* she seeks both solace and sanctuary just like Buddhist inmate Jarvis Jay Masters when he transforms his San Quentin death row prison cell into a temple. Similarly, Starhawk, a pagan, desires comfort and a renewed sense of rightness as she helps restore order to a Palestinian home ransacked by Israeli soldiers. When you start seeking the connections instead of the differences among the selections in *Next to Godliness*, you'll find they dovetail quite naturally.

It's always easier to start with the small to learn about the large. A lowercase "a" must be mastered before a novel can be written, and so it is with the sacrament of cleaning. The structure of *Next to God-liness* progresses from the minor and literally contained (a sink full of dishes, a hamper of laundry) to the almost too vast to be genuinely comprehensible—disastrous messes like war and hurricanes that are inflicted on our world by humans and nature. Just as daily meditation practice or the ritual of morning prayer ready us for the spiritual challenges we face in our lives, exploring the minute aspects of cleaning—the common rituals of tidying up, sweeping, and launder-ing our clothes—expands to apply to our home lives, our work lives, and ultimately our community and our planet. In other words, by rinsing a dish with genuine focus we prepare ourselves for enormous spiritual challenges and symbolically take care of the universal things, like the cyclical international disasters of war and pollution— metaphorically expressed as "Laundry" by Allen Ginsberg in *Homework*—or the loss of a loved one to the slow and insidious effects of witnessing the cruelties of war, like the grandfather in Eric Leigh's *Last of the Midnight Lullabies*. Likewise, as Rengetsu shows us in *Removing the Soot* and Rabbi Lynn Gottlieb writes in her poem about cleaning in anticipation of Pesach, wholeheartedly dusting something informs the experience and great possibilities symbolized in celebrating a festive occasion with our communities.

Next to Godliness* is not a textbook. It is not an authoritative volume on housecleaning or comparative religion. I am an expert in neither cleaning nor religion, but in addition to finding comfort in cleaning, I have always been a spiritual seeker and a hungry reader of literature of all and every faith. I constantly respond to the places where seemingly disparate belief systems express the same thing using different metaphors or mythologies. From that place of quiet, intro-spective inquiry, it was a natural step to compile this book, as I gath-ered literary passages where housekeeping and religion connect and where I believe the connection will resonate for you, the reader.

This collection is less an anthology and more a commonplace book—a wonderful old-fashioned term that is enjoying a revival thanks to blogging. Robert Darnton gave an eloquent explanation of commonplace books in an article in *The New York Review of Books* ("Extraordinary Commonplaces," December 21, 2000) when he wrote:

> *Time was when readers kept commonplace books.*
> *Whenever they came across a pithy passage, they*
> *copied it into a notebook under an appropriate head-*
> *ing, adding observations made in the course of daily*
> *life. Erasmus instructed them how to do it ... The*
> *practice spread everywhere in early modern Eng-*
> *land, among ordinary readers as well as famous*
> *writers like Francis Bacon, Ben Jonson, John Mil-*
> *ton, and John Locke. It involved a special way of*
> *taking in the printed word. Unlike modern readers,*
> *who follow the flow of a narrative from beginning to*
> *end, early modern Englishmen read in fits and starts*
> *and jumped from book to book. They broke texts*
> *into fragments and assembled them into new pat-*
> *terns by transcribing them in different sections of*
> *their notebooks. Then they reread the copies and*
> *rearranged the patterns while adding more excerpts.*
> *Reading and writing were therefore inseparable*
> *activities. They belonged to a continuous effort to*
> *make sense of things."*

And this is what I've done—I've read and subjectively excerpted pieces from all kinds of books and authors and organized them in a way that speaks about the process of using mundane, repetitious, and not always pleasurable ritual to experience something that is at best transcendent—like the peaceful world Stephen Vincent Benét visualizes in his "Prayer" or what the grandmother experiences while "performing the rituals of the ordinary as an act of faith" in Marilynne Robinson's *Housekeeping*—or at least comforting, like the friendship Gunilla Norris finds with her broom or the purity Pablo Neruda sees rising from the soap suds. The more I looked, the more links between clean and holy I found—links that bridge faiths, politics, gender, nationality, and history.

Further to my "continuous effort to make sense of things," you will see that I open each section of the book with brief reflections—

notes on the subject at hand. These section introductions can serve as bookmarks. I've also taken the liberty of giving titles to the passages that didn't already have them. There is no science to this entitling. The naming is more a distillation, for me, of the content of a piece in terms of the book. My hope is that these titles will not strike you as random, but, rather, that they will work as a series of signposts in navigating the writings in a section.

Clearly, cleaning isn't always a holy experience. I've consciously avoided vast and critical issues of feminism, toxins, and labor injustices—but there are times when bettering your physical, external surroundings can make you better and positively affect and impact your spiritual, internal self. In other words, there are times when the simple, methodical actions of housekeeping truly contribute to a sense of order, accomplishment, and well-being.

Through the writings gathered in this book, I've witnessed some of those moments when cleaning becomes a process of creating a consecrated place in our everyday lives, a sacrament of homemaking, a clarifying power of doing something wholly and wholly well … the poetry of order and cleanliness. I hope you will too. Perhaps you'll even find a piece in this collection that moves you to begin a commonplace book of your own.

I long to accomplish a great and noble task, but it is my chief duty to accomplish small tasks as if they were great and noble.

—Helen Keller

PART ONE

Washing the Dishes

My grandmother used to joke that she didn't need to buy a dishwasher. Why spend the money, when she had my grandfather? He did the dishes after every meal, and his books about Buddhism and esoteric philosophy were also the first ones I read, the beginnings of my library and my fascination. Coincidence?

The simple act of washing dishes has compelled writers from all eras and religious traditions to consider the meaning beyond their actions. From Thich Nhat Hanh's Buddhist monastery to Brother Lawrence's seventeenth-century French abbey to Dominique Browning revisiting her grandparents' Kentucky farmhouse, this timeless task has motivated people toward discovery of the peaceful and profound.

Washing the dishes is both a beginning and an ending. Thich Nhat Hanh observes that, "we do the dishes in order to have clean dishes, we also do the dishes just to do the dishes" which allows for true presence and ultimate awareness in those moments of washing.

To contemplate self-discovery and find times of transcendence in a sink overflowing with dishes may take some effort. After all, washing the dishes is rote, mundane—you may even think of it as menial. Yet isn't that the beauty of it? Much like the rhythmic pulse of a mantra, the repetitive action of washing a plate, a bowl, a cup can clear our minds, calm our spirits, and bring us into the present. As the water rinses away the food remnants from a pan, we can allow this act to rinse away the debris of our day, to "leave no trace," as Bernard Glassman and Rick Fields convey. Our minds are open to experience awe, serenity, peace.

Taigu Ryokan, a Buddhist monk from Japan known for his pure observations, demonstrates the similarities between the sounds of washing and sounds in nature. His succinct poem encourages us to reflect and to question: If Ryokan had not been fully present at the moment he listened, would he have been able to make his comparison? How many times have we absently scrubbed a dish, wishing we were somewhere, anywhere, else? What might we discover if we arrive at the moment, ready to be in that moment, as Ryokan was?

Dominique Browning offers a response to these questions in a more straightforward, but no less poignant way. She frankly admits, "Every gadget that promises a cleaner house, a better dish, is something I want in my life." Only after she witnesses a friend enjoying the process of cleaning up after a party is Browning prompted to wonder, "What have we lost in all the acquiring?" of designer appliances and faster, shinier, ultra-efficient tools. Browning considers the tangible closeness and love between her grandparents (who, like mine, never owned a dishwasher) as she remembers them standing at their sink, slowly washing and drying the dishes and, in those moments of ultimate being, creating a home together.

Through musings on washing dishes we can explore the very essence of a simple task; we discover that each time we pick up a sponge we are faced with choices: we can truly show up for the moment of washing, or risk losing that moment forever.

Thich Nhat Hanh

"Bathing a Newborn Buddha"

To my mind, the idea that doing dishes is unpleasant can occur only when you aren't doing them. Once you are standing in front of the sink with your sleeves rolled up and your hands in warm water, it really isn't so bad. I enjoy taking my time with each dish, being fully aware of the dish, the water, and each movement of my hands. I know that if I hurry in order to go and have a cup of tea, the time will be unpleasant, and not worth living. That would be a pity, for each minute, each second of life is a miracle. The dishes themselves and the fact that I am here washing them are miracles! Each bowl I wash, each poem I compose, each time I invite a bell to sound is a miracle, and each has exactly the same value. One day, while washing a bowl, I felt that my movements were as sacred and respectful as bathing a newborn Buddha. If he were to read this, that newborn Buddha would certainly be happy for me, and not at all insulted at being compared with a bowl.

Each thought, each action in the sunlight of awareness becomes sacred. In this light, no boundary exists between the sacred and the profane. I must confess it takes me a bit longer to do the dishes, but I live fully in every moment, and I am happy. Washing the dishes is at the same time a means and an end—that is, not only do we do the dishes in order to have clean dishes, we also do the dishes just to do the dishes, to live fully in each moment while washing them.

If I am incapable of washing dishes joyfully, if I want to finish them quickly so I can go and have a cup of tea, I will be equally incapable of drinking the tea joyfully. With the cup in my hands I will be thinking about what to do next, and the fragrance and the flavor of the tea, together with the pleasure of drinking it, will be lost. I will always be dragged into the future, never able to live in the present moment.

Brother Lawrence

SACRAMENT

Lord of all pots and pans and things …
Make me a saint by getting meals
And washing up the plates!

[Brother Lawrence] discoursed with [the Abbott Joseph de Beaufort] frequently … and with great openness of heart, concerning his manner of *going* to God….

That in the beginning of his novitiate he spent the hours appointed for private prayer in thinking of God, so as to convince his mind of, and to impress deeply upon his heart, the divine existence, rather by devout sentiments, and submission to the lights of faith, than by studied reasoning and elaborate meditations. That by this short and sure method he exercised himself in the knowledge and love of God, resolving to use his utmost endeavor to live in a continual sense of His presence, and, if possible never to forget Him more.

That when he had thus in prayer filled his mind with great sentiments of that infinite being, he went to his work appointed in the kitchen (for he was cook to the society). There having first considered severally the things his office required, and when and how each thing was to be done, he spent all the intervals of his time, as well before as after his work, in prayer.

That when he began his business, he said to God, with a filial trust in Him: *O my God, since Thou art with me, and I must now, in obedience to Thy commands, apply my mind to these outward things, I beseech Thee to grant me the grace to continue in Thy presence; and to this end do Thou prosper me with Thy assistance, receive all my works, and possess all my affections.*

As he proceeded in his work he continued his familiar conversation with his Maker, imploring His grace, and offering to Him all actions.

When he had finished he examined himself how he had discharged his duty; if he found *well*, he returned thanks to God; if otherwise, he asked pardon, and, without being discouraged, he set his mind right again, and continued his exercise of the *presence* of God as if he had never deviated from it. "Thus," said he, "by rising after my falls, and by frequently renewed acts of faith and love, I am come to a state wherein it would be as difficult for me not to think of God as it was at first to accustom myself to it."

As Brother Lawrence had found such an advantage in walking in the presence of God, it was natural for him to recommend it earnestly to others; but his example was a stronger inducement than any arguments he could propose. His very countenance was edifying, such a sweet and calm devotion appearing in it as could not but affect the beholders. And it was observed that in the greatest hurry of business in the kitchen he still preserved his recollection and heavenly-mindedness. He was never hasty nor loitering, but did each thing in its season, with an even, uninterrupted composure and tranquility of spirit. "The time of business," said he, "does not with me differ from the time of prayer; and in the noise and clatter of my kitchen, while several persons are at the same time calling for different things, I possess God in as great tranquility as if I were upon my knees at the blessed sacrament."

Taigu Ryokan

CADENCE

The sound of the woman scouring
the cook pot
blends with the sound of the frog.

Dominique Browning

"DOING THE DISHES"

One evening I was talking to a friend as he bustled around, clearing the table and washing the dishes after a dinner he had prepared for a rather large group. He seemed to enjoy the cleanup as much as he had the cooking—soaping each plate, glass, and pot lavishly, rinsing it thoroughly and placing it to dry on a rack. I asked him why all this seemed to give him so much pleasure. "It's my way of saying thank you to the pot," he replied, patting its bottom as tenderly as if he had just diapered a baby.

No dishwasher. No caterer. No maid. Preparation, cooking, serving—all accomplished in a spirit of steady, patient, and companionable effort. Of course, everything we build into our kitchens today goes in the opposite direction. Several dishwashers. Caterer's kitchens. Enough refrigerators to set the house humming. We need all the help we can get. Every gadget that promises a cleaner house, a better dish, is something I want in my life. I am always turning down the corners of pages in the Williams-Sonoma catalog in search of the elusive tool for better—best!—living.

It has been ever thus; our enthusiasm for the things that make housework easier isn't new. Each generation finds its own tools for liberation. And buying these things for someone else is even considered a mark of love, affection, and solidarity in the mutual assault on homemaking. ("And he bought her a dishwasher and a coffee percolator ... " as Joni Mitchell traces the arc of a love affair.) Myself, I can't wait to buy a brand-new, super-quiet, elegant dishwasher whose door won't need slamming five or six times to convince it that I'm seriously ready to get this load done.

But what have we lost in all the acquiring? Some attitude of caring for, of gratitude for, the things that make up the everyday rituals of life. One of my fondest childhood memories is of enormous Sunday meals with my grandparents in Kentucky, a place we never visited often enough, as far as I was concerned. I loved everything about it—the simple white clapboard house, the sleeping porch where I was placed in a cot so high off the ground I had to be lifted out of bed in the morning, the farm, the cows, the little pond where I caught my first fish, my grandfather's fragrant pipe, my grandmother's radiantly sweet soul.

My grandparents served elaborate dinners after the Sunday church service, huge affairs, aunts, uncles, cousins gathered around a table piled high (in my child's eye) with chicken and mashed potatoes and greens and gravy and biscuits. And corn bread. Thick fragrant butter. Heavy sweet milk. Pecan pie and chocolate cake always followed, with ice cream. Well, at least that's how I remember those feasts. One treat after another spooling down the length of the table. Afterward, my grandparents would head into the kitchen to clean up.

Many years later, long after they had died, my father made a remark, almost offhandedly, probably during one of our incessant arguments about whose turn it was to do the dishes, about how his parents had never even owned a dishwasher, so who was I to complain? When my dad had urged them to "modernize," they refused. Cleaning up after meals was a pleasure to them. There was nothing he liked more, my grandfather explained, than standing next to my grandmother after dinner while she washed the dishes and handed them, one by one, to him to pat dry and put away. They loved each other. What more could they want? Together, they made a home.

Bernard Glassman
and Rick Fields

"Clearing the Table"

There is a koan about a monk who comes to the Zen master Joshu and says, "Please give me a practice."

And Joshu says, "Have you eaten your meal?" Which means, in Zen talk, "Have you tasted enlightenment?"

The monk says, "Yes, I have eaten a meal."

"Good," Joshu says. "Then go wash your bowls."

Joshu's "wash your bowls" was pointing out that enlightenment should not leave a trace. But he was also pointing out that it is very difficult, if not impossible, to eliminate all traces. It's like the tortoise in another Zen story. The tortoise always leaves footprints on the sand. And then the tortoise's tail wipes away the footprints. But then the tortoise's tail leaves tail prints!

So it's almost impossible to eliminate all our traces. We may eat all our food, clean the counters, wash the dishes, and scrub the pots. But then we have to wipe the soap off the counters, and clean the sinks, and then we find ourselves left with dirty sponges, and as we look back, we notice that we've tracked some of the dirty water on the clean kitchen floor.

In the same way, we drop the conditioning or attitude that keeps us separated from the next thing, that very process creates a certain amount of conditioning, and then *that* has to be dropped away too.

Joshu's "wash your bowls" is about this process. Even though it may not be possible, we should try to leave no trace of what we've done. Therefore we don't walk around saying, "I've been enlightened," or "I've made this great product." If our enlightenment is genuine, it will express itself in the way we act in ordinary life.

In the Zen monastery, after the monks have eaten everything that's in their bowls, they clean the bowls with tea or plain hot water. Then they drink the water. The water that's left over in the bowls goes back into the gardens.

This traceless "nothing left over" has a very profound spiritual meaning, but it also has a very practical ecological application. If there's any trace left over, it should be used again—and again until nothing is left over. If you're a manufacturer you have to take into account what happens to a product after it is used up. You have to think about how your product will go away. Whether you create a new car, a new refrigerator, or a new cookie tin, you have to create a way for your creation to be recycled.

If you do that, if you get rid of the traces of the car you've built, or the wonderful banquet you've just eaten, you open up the space so that you can see a whole new set of ingredients. So eliminating the traces is really another way of saying we're cleaning up, which is where we began.

Leaving no trace is what Zen calls "non-duality." Subject and object collapse. The distinction between the helper and those who are being helped disappears, as does the distinction between giver and gift, or cook and guest.

Actually, [Zen master] Dogen doesn't suggest that we cook our whole meal and then clean up at the end. He tells us that no trace should happen *as* we're doing it—so that nobody knows what we've done.

So we clean up while we're cooking. We eliminate traces as we go. And yet at the end there's still a stage of cleaning up, just as there is at the beginning. Although we've created that stage of no-trace, although we're going to start all over—we still start with cleaning up, even if we walk in and everything looks clean already. Even though we may feel very calm, in a deep state of concentration, the way of the Zen cook is to always start with a little centering and return to Beginner's Mind so that we can clean up and take stock of our ingredients.

And now we're ready to begin again.

PART TWO

Laundry

Laundry can be seen as a metaphor for our spiritual journey. When we wash our clothes we have the opportunity to take something soiled and return it to its original purity—a new beginning. For me, when the world is overwhelming, there's no comfort quite like ironing and getting to approach perfection by easing the wrinkles out.

Often, doing the laundry—washing, drying, sorting, pressing, folding—is simply another duty on the long list of household chores, but pause to consider the elements of this ostensibly mundane task that have been passed down from generations before us, and the task of doing laundry shifts from menial to a ritualized practice surviving years of successes and hardships, struggles and triumphs, births and deaths. We can witness the process of transformation as well. Laundry can be an expression of a new beginning, from dirty to clean, imperfection to purity.

Laundry is universal. Kathleen Norris, a poet and oblate of Assumption Abbey in rural North Dakota, points out that when we stop to consider the "democratic" nature of the act of doing laundry, we discover a commonality we share with everyone from television commentators to Benedictine nuns—we all have to do it. When we look at the process through Norris's eyes, we see that laundry is indeed a universal task that can renew our connection to the actions, history, and intentions of members of our own families. This bond is nurtured not only through the tangible aspects of washing clothes—Norris's grandmother's bottles of bluing remain in her basement—but also in the methods of doing laundry—Norris celebrates spring's return by hanging the first laundry of the season on the line, just as her mother used to.

The many stages in the process of doing laundry offer us ample time for reflection, allowing for moments of meditation and the opportunity to encounter memories and emotions that may get buried as we go through our days. It is through these "rituals of the ordinary" that Marilynne Robinson examines longing and sadness, reflected upon during the process of washing and hanging out the laundry. In these reflections we see a lineage of women (just as we do in Norris's piece) propelled by "the resurrection of the ordinary"—the cyclic, expected occurrence of spring and all that comes with it. When we explore doing laundry from this perspective—as a symbol of winter's end and the restoration of a ritual that encourages contemplation—it becomes something other than drudgery, it becomes a way of rejoicing.

If we look at washing our clothes as a symbol for cleaning up our world, we can discover the ways that this simple act contributes to a sense of hope. Chilean statesman and poet Pablo Neruda takes the metaphor of laundry and stretches it beyond the clothesline to encompass the planet when he celebrates the possibilities in washing out the "combat" in linen, canvas, and calico only to discover that "purity comes back from the soap suds." In other words, in dirtiness lies the opportunity for cleanliness, as long as there are hands to continue "mak[ing] the world every day."

The ritualized act of doing laundry, much like the rituals of our faith practices, can represent comfort and security. In the excerpt from James Baldwin's *Go Tell It on the Mountain*, the act of doing the laundry provides a familiar setting for a mother and son to have an emotionally charged conversation. The mother channels her nervous energy through her hands—so familiar is this routine that her body is able to perform these actions without her thinking—and her

laundry posture allows her a convenient target on which to focus—
or perhaps avert—her gaze. The boy takes comfort in the familiar
sight of his mother's actions and appearance—the spot on the waist
of her apron, her pose as she stands over the washtub, the sweat on
her forehead. They both find safety in this physical setting that
they know so well, as their minds and hearts move forward into the
unknown, an intimate and awkward discussion of the future. The act
of washing clothes becomes not a backdrop, but an integral part of
the conversation itself. If it were not for the safety the ritualized act
of doing laundry offers, we can wonder if their conversation would
have taken place at all.

Exploring the act of washing our clothes and the sense of satisfaction many of us feel at its completion may inspire us to see the
process as an art form, encouraging us to look for means of self-
expression through performing this simple chore. Polish-born American author Anzia Yezierska approaches laundry as just that, creating a
milieu where the task of doing the laundry becomes a mode of creativity, a window into beauty, love, and friendship—a way to "consider the nature of the things before you," as Buddhist Gary Thorp
writes.

It may seem a bit of a cognitive leap to think of laundry as the
stuff of poetry, but in his classic American hymn of laundry and life,
"Love Calls Us to the Things of This World," poet Richard Wilbur
articulates how clean clothes and holiness are one and the same
when embodied by the human rapture of laundry on a line. Wilbur
celebrates these "clear dances done in the sight of heaven" showing
the relationship between laundry and life, allowing us to awaken ourselves to the beauty surrounding us.

In the selections that follow, laundry evokes angels and purity,
comfort and resurrection. Washing clothes becomes more than a
metaphor—it becomes a sacred process unto itself.

Kathleen Norris

"AT LAST, HER LAUNDRY'S DONE"

Laundry seems to have an almost religious importance for many women. We groan about the drudgery but seldom talk about the secret pleasure we feel at being able to make dirty things clean, especially the clothes of our loved ones, which possess an intimacy all their own. Laundry is one of the very few tasks in life that offers instant results, and this is nothing to sneer at. It's also democratic; everyone has to do it, or figure out a way to get it done. When I picture Honolulu's Chinatown, circa 1960, which I passed through daily on a school bus, what I smell is the open-air fish market, but what I see are the signs, mysterious to me then, that read "Taxi Dance Hall: Girls Wanted," and all the colorful laundry strung up between tenements. There was never a day without it. In any city slum, it's laundry—neat lines of babies' T-shirts, kids' underwear and jeans—that announces that families live here, and that someone cares. For some people, laundry seems to satisfy a need for ritual. A television commentator with a hectic schedule once told me that the best, most contemplative part of his day was early morning, a time he set aside for laundering and ironing his shirts.

My images of laundry abound. One that I've never seen but love to imagine is that of Benedictine nuns in the Dakotas, in the days before Vatican II, when many of them worked in elementary schools, beating their black serge habits on snow banks to get the dust out.

They tell me that the snow was good for removing stains. I picture the small clothesline that a friend has put up in her penthouse garden in Manhattan. For her, laundry is a triumph of hope over experience. "I grew up in the suburbs," she explains, "and my mother hung clothes on the line. This is not ideal," she admits, "but on a nice windy day, the soot doesn't fall."

Of course an attachment to laundry can be pathetic, even pathological, in a woman who feels that it's one of the few areas in her life over which she has control. More often, though, it's an affectionate throwback to the world of our mothers and grandmothers. We may be businesswomen or professors, but it's hard to shake that urge to do laundry "the right way," just like mama did. The sense that "laundry must not be done casually," as an arts administrator once told me, is something that seems lost on most men. She and her husband had reached an armed truce: he could do his own laundry but was to leave hers alone. She had grown tired of picking lint from his red sweatpants off her good blouses.

Many women have a "system" that is not to be trifled with. "You're hanging the underwear wrong" I was solemnly informed by a woman minister one day as we rushed to get her laundry on the line so that we could get to a meeting. She had a Master of Divinity degree from Princeton Seminary, but that's not where she learned that only a slouch would dare to use a dryer on a fine, windy summer day such as this in Lemmon, South Dakota, or that the fact was so obvious it could remain unspoken between us. She relegated me to the simple stuff, pillowcases and towels, but she kept an eye on me.

At St. John's [Abbey and University in Collegeville, Minnesota] we had been housed in a block of small, elegant, but very livable apartments designed by Marcel Breuer, and clotheslines were not permitted. The great architect found them "tacky," we were told, and visually distracting. It is good to be home, where I can hang clothes and air bedding on the line, and be as tacky as I like. I come by my attachment to laundry honestly. One of my first visual memories is of my mother pulling clothes from the sky; she had a line on a pulley that ran from a window in our row house near the Naval gunnery in Washington, D.C. These days, my mother lives in a neighborhood in Honolulu where her backyard clothesline is something of a scandal. But she's a Plainswoman at heart, and a clothesline is simple necessity.

Living in the house where she grew up, I've become pleasantly haunted by laundry. I'm grateful that I no longer have to pull clothes through a wringer, as my grandmother did for years. Her bottles of bluing gather dust in the basement; I haven't used them, but can't throw them out. But, like her, I wouldn't dream of using the electric dryer unless I have to. In March or April I begin to long for the day when I can hang clothes on the line again. Our winters are so long and severe in western South Dakota that we bank on the slightest summer joys; the scent of clothes dried out of doors, the sweet smell of sun on them.

I must be vigilant; sudden thunderstorms march across the prairie in late afternoon, making a mockery of clothes hung out to dry. Our winds can be so strong that clothes go flying. And during times of drought, there is sometimes so much dust in the air that line drying is impractical. Old-timers who recall the "Dirty Thirties" speak of seeing grasshoppers eat clothes right off the line, a sight I never hope to see, although I've thought about it in the springs and summers when we've waited months for rain.

My youngest sister once had a dream about a tornado that seemed an astute portrait of our parents: as the storm approached, Dad wandered off to get a better look at the twister and Mom ran to get the clothes off the line. I recall running into my clergy friend one evening at a church supper. She'd been frantically busy with meetings all day and the next night would be conducting a wedding rehearsal. News of a death in the congregation meant that she now also had a funeral to prepare for, and this led us to talk of epitaphs. "I know what I want on my tombstone," she said. "At last, her laundry's done."

Pablo Neruda

"An Ode for Ironing"

Poetry is white
it comes dripping out of the water
it gets wrinkled and piles up
We have to stretch out the skin of this planet
We have to iron the sea in its whiteness
The hands go on and on
and so things are made
the hands make the world every day
fire unites with steel
linen, canvas and calico come back
from combat in the laundry
and from the light a dove is born
purity comes back from the soap suds.

James Baldwin

BIRTHDAY

When he had finished and the room was ready for Sunday, John felt dusty and weary and sat down beside the window in his father's easy chair....

But now it was eleven o'clock, and in two hours his father would be home. And then they might eat, and then his father would lead them in prayer, and then he would give them a Bible lesson. By and by it would be evening and he would go to clean the church, and remain for tarry service. Suddenly, sitting at the window, and with a violence unprecedented, there arose in John a flood of fury and tears, and he bowed his head, fists clenched against the windowpane, crying, with teeth on edge: "What shall I do? What shall I do?"

Then his mother called him; and he remembered that she was in the kitchen washing clothes and probably had something for him to do. He rose sullenly and walked into the kitchen. She stood over the washtub, her arms wet and soapy to the elbows and sweat standing on her brow. Her apron, improvised from an old sheet, was wet where she had been leaning over the scrubbing-board. As he came in, she straightened, drying her hands on the edge of the apron.

"You finish your work, John?" she asked.

He said: "Yes'm," and thought how oddly she looked at him; as though she were looking at someone else's child.

"That's a good boy," she said. She smiled a shy, strained smile. "You know you your mother's right-hand man?"

He said nothing, and he did not smile, but watched her, wondering to what task this preamble led.

She turned away, passing one damp hand across her forehead, and went to the cupboard. Her back was to him, and he watched her while she took down a bright, figured vase, filled with flowers only on the most special occasions, and emptied the contents into her palm. He heard the chink of money, which meant that she was going to send him to the store. She put the vase back and turned to face him, her palm loosely folded before her.

"I didn't never ask you," she said, "what you wanted for your birthday. But you take this, son, and go out and get yourself something you think you want."

And she opened his palm and put the money into it, warm and wet from her hand. In the moment that he felt the warm, smooth coins and her hand on his, John stared blindly at her face, so far above him. His heart broke and he wanted to put his head on her belly where the wet spot was, and cry. But he dropped his eyes and looked at his palm, at the small pile of coins.

"It ain't much there," she said.

"That's all right." Then he looked up, and she bent down and kissed him on the forehead.

"You getting to be," she said, putting her hand beneath his chin and holding his face away from her, "a right big boy. You going to be a mighty fine man, you know that? Your mama's counting on you."

And he knew again that she was not saying everything she meant; in a kind of secret language she was telling him today something that he must remember and understand tomorrow. He watched her face, his heart swollen with love for her and with an anguish, not yet his own, that he did not understand and that frightened him.

"Yes, Ma," he said, hoping that she would realize, despite his stammering tongue, the depth of his passion to please her.

"I know," she said, with a smile, releasing him and rising, "there's a whole lot of things you don't understand. But don't you fret. The Lord'll reveal to you in His own good time everything He wants you to know. You put your faith in the Lord, Johnny, and He'll surely bring you out. Everything works together for good for them that love the Lord."

He had heard her say this before—it was her text, as *Set thine house in order* was his father's—but he knew that today she was saying it to him especially; she was trying to help him because she knew he was in trouble. And this trouble was also her own, which she would never tell to John. And even though he was certain that they could not be speaking of the same thing—for then, surely, she would be angry and no longer proud of him—this perception on her part and this avowal of her love for him lent to John's bewilderment a reality that terrified and a dignity that consoled him. Dimly, he felt that he ought to console her, and he listened, astounded, at the words that now fell from his lips:

"Yes, Mama. I'm going to try to love the Lord."

At this there sprang into his mother's face something startling, beautiful, unspeakably sad—as though she were looking far beyond him at a long, dark road, and seeing on that road a traveler in perpetual danger. Was it he, the traveler? or herself? or was she thinking of the cross of Jesus? She turned back to the washtub, still with this strange sadness on her face.

Marilynne Robinson

RESURRECTION OF THE ORDINARY

One day my grandmother must have carried out a basket of sheets to hang in the spring sunlight, wearing her widow's black, performing the rituals of the ordinary as an act of faith. Say there were two or three inches of hard old snow on the ground, with earth here and there oozing through the broken places, and that there was warmth in the sunlight, when the wind did not blow it all away, and say she stooped breathlessly in her corset to lift up a sodden sheet by its hems, and say that when she had pinned three corners to the lines it began to billow and leap in her hands, to flutter and tremble, and to glare with the light, and that the throes of the thing were as gleeful and strong as if a spirit were dancing in its cerements. That wind! She would say, because it pushed the skirts of her coat against her legs and made strands of her hair fly. It came down the lake, and it smelled sweetly of snow, and rankly of melting snow, and it called to mind the small, scarce, stemmy flowers that she and Edmund would walk half a day to pick, though in another day they would all be wilted. Sometimes Edmund would carry buckets and a trowel, and lift them earth and all, and bring them home to plant, and they would die. They were rare things, and grew out of ants' nests and bear dung and the flesh of perished animals. She and Edmund would climb until they were wet with sweat. Horseflies followed them, and the wind

24

chilled them. Where the snow receded, they might see the ruins of a porcupine, teeth here, tail there. The wind would be sour with stale snow and death and pine pitch and wildflowers.

In a month those flowers would bloom. In a month all dormant life and arrested decay would begin again.

In a month she would not mourn, because in that season it had never seemed to her that they were married, she and the silent Methodist Edmund who wore a necktie and suspenders even to hunt wildflowers, and who remembered just where they grew from year to year, and who dipped his handkerchief in a puddle to wrap the stems, and who put out his elbow to help her over the steep and stony places, with a wordless and impersonal courtesy she did not resent because she had never really wished to feel married to anyone. She sometimes imagined a rather dark man with crude stripes painted on his face and sunken belly, and a hide fastened around his loins, and bones dangling from his ears, and clay and claws and fangs and bones and feathers and sinews and hide ornamenting his arms and waist and throat and ankles, his whole body a boast that he was more alarming than all the death whose trophies he wore. Edmund was like that, a little. The rising of the spring stirred a serious, mystical excitement in him, and made him forgetful of her. He would pick up eggshells, a bird's wing, a jawbone, the ashy fragment of a wasp's nest. He would peer at each of them with the most absolute attention, and then put them in his pockets, where he kept his jackknife and his loose change. He would peer at them as if he could read them, and pocket them as if he could own them. This is death in my hand, this is ruin in my breast pocket, where I keep my reading glasses. At such times he was as forgetful of her as he was of his suspenders and his Methodism, but all the same it was then that she loved him best, as a soul all unaccompanied, like her own.

So the wind that billowed her sheets announced to her the resurrection of the ordinary. Soon the skunk cabbage would come up, and the cidery smell would rise in the orchard, and the girls would wash and starch and iron their cotton dresses. And every evening would bring its familiar strangeness, and crickets would sing the whole night long, under her windows and in every part of the black wilderness that stretched away from Fingerbone on every side. And she would feel that sharp loneliness she had felt every long evening since she was a child. It was the kind of loneliness that made clocks seem slow and loud and made voices sound like voices across water. Old women she had known, first her grandmother and then her mother, rocked on their porches in the evenings and sang sad songs, and did not wish to be spoken to.

Anzia Yezierska

ARTIST

"Amen!" breathed Hanneh Hayyeh. "May we all forget from our worries for rent!"

Mrs. Preston followed with keen delight Hanneh Hayyeh's every movement as she lifted the wash from the basket and spread it on the bed. Hanneh Hayyeh's rough, toil-worn hands lingered lovingly, caressingly over each garment. It was as though the fabrics held something subtly animate in their texture that penetrated to her very fingertips.

"Hanneh Hayyeh! You're an artist!" There was reverence in Mrs. Preston's low voice that pierced the other woman's inmost being. "You do my laces and batistes as no one else ever has. It's as if you breathed part of your soul into it."

The hungry-eyed, ghetto woman drank in thirstily the beauty and goodness that radiated from Mrs. Preston's person. None of the cultured elegance of her adored friend escaped Hanneh Hayyeh. Her glance traveled from the exquisite shoes to the flawless hair of the well-poised head.

"Your things got so much fineness. I'm crazy for the feel from them. I do them up so light in my hands like it was thin air I was handling."

Hanneh Hayyeh pantomimed as she spoke and Mrs. Preston, roused from her habitual reserve, put her fine, white hand affectionately over Hanneh Hayyeh's gnarled, roughened ones.

"Oi-i-i-i! Mrs. Preston! You always make me feel so grand!" said Hanneh Hayyeh, a mist of tears in her wistful eyes. "When I go away from you I could just sit down and cry. I can't give it out in words what it is. It chokes me so – how good you are to me – You ain't at all like a rich lady. You're so plain from the heart. You make the lowest nobody feel he's somebody."

"You are not a 'nobody,' Hanneh Hayyeh. You are an artist—an artist laundress."

"What mean you an artist?"

"An artist is so filled with love for the beautiful that he has to express it in some way. You express it in your washing just as a painter paints it in a picture."

Gary Thorp

INTEGRATIVE PRACTICE

As you do these everyday chores around the house, you have the perfect opportunity to engage in what some people refer to as integrative practice. This is just another way of saying that you try to bring the qualities of zazen, sitting meditation, into your everyday activities. The laundry or washroom offers another venue where you can experience this practice. It's just as natural for us to clean and care for the clothes we wear as it is for an egret to preen his feathers or for a house cat to lick her fur in the sunshine. Most people these days don't have to beat their clothing against river rocks or rinse them in their drinking pools. Doing the laundry can in fact be a very pleasant experience; it's a great chance to enjoy a feeling of renewal. Consider the warmth of the laundry that comes out of the dryer, the feel of each item as you fold it. If you use a clothesline to dry your laundry, you can also marvel at the warmth of the sun and the release of moisture into the air. Savor the aroma of freshness in the things you have washed. Consider the nature of the things before you and of those who made them available.

In formal Zen practice, there are explicit instructions on how to care for one's robes and bedding. Each item is handled in a certain way, washed in a certain way, and stored in a certain way, all handed down through the centuries from teacher to student. These small rituals have a twofold purpose: They help ensure uniformity and equality in the monastery setting, and they also help residents focus their attention on what they're doing. The point is not to do things quickly but to do them completely.

Today, we often sacrifice many of life's experiences for the sake of speed. We're constantly short of time, no matter how much time we have. We're continually preparing for and rushing to meet "something." What this "something" is, we often don't know. We only know that we have to be ready for it, and the sooner we escape from what it is we are doing, the better. But once we step back a bit and begin to look at things more carefully, we can begin asking the questions of ourselves that can instruct our lives.

Even when confronted with the most modern and shining coin-operated machines at the Laundromat, you can find the subtle questions and teachings of Zen. But sometimes it is best not to take these questions and symbols so seriously. After all, just how permanent is "permanent press"? And what about the machine on the wall dispensing "change"? You can view the spinning drums of the commercial dryers as prayer wheels, or wheels of Samsara. You can ask if bleach will really make white things whiter, or if the "gentle cycle" makes the machine become more compassionate. And what should you do when your entire load of washing becomes "unbalanced"?

Just do your laundry and try not to identify yourself too much with your own clothing. As Suzuki Roshi said, we sometimes talk about the clothes we wear, and we sometimes talk about our human bodies, but neither of these is really what we are. We are "the big activity." This big activity can also be the small activity. It can be the loose button bouncing against the leg of the table. It can be the mending and patching of clothing, the washing of one's work clothes, or the smell of clean socks folded in a drawer. It can often be as simple as hearing the sound of water dripping on other water.

Richard Wilbur

"LOVE CALLS US TO THE THINGS OF THIS WORLD"

The eyes open to a cry of pulleys,
And spirited from sleep, the astounded soul
Hangs for a moment bodiless and simple
As false dawn.
                    Outside the open window
The morning air is all awash with angels.

    Some are in bed-sheets, some are in blouses,
Some are in smocks: but truly there they are.
Now they are rising together in calm swells
Of halcyon feeling, filling whatever they wear
With the deep joy of their impersonal breathing;

    Now they are flying in place, conveying
The terrible speed of their omnipresence, moving
And staying like white water; and now of a sudden
They swoon down into so rapt a quiet
That nobody seems to be there.
                    The soul shrinks

From all that it is about to remember,
From the punctual rape of every blessèd day,
And cries,

        "Oh, let there be nothing on earth but laundry,
Nothing but rosy hands in the rising steam
And clear dances done in the sight of heaven."

Yet, as the sun acknowledges
With a warm look the world's hunks and colors,
The soul descends once more in bitter love
To accept the waking body, saying now
In a changed voice as the man yawns and rises,
        "Bring them down from their ruddy gallows;
Let there be clean linen for the backs of thieves;
Let lovers go fresh and sweet to be undone,
And the heaviest nuns walk in a pure floating
Of dark habits,

            keeping their difficult balance."

Part Three

Sweeping

Looking at sweeping as something other than a never-ending chore affords us the opportunity to see in ourselves the infinite possibility that can be discovered in every action, word, and gesture.

Unlike laundry—a job that has a start and a finish—sweeping is never quite finished. Once you've swept, there remain traces of the sweeping to do away with, and no end to dust. Through the repetition of the task, we learn that there will always be more to sweep. From this perspective, we can immerse ourselves in the process, seeing beyond the back-and-forth movements of the broom into acts of service and lovingkindness. By paying attention to the path that a broom cuts through dirt on a floor, we can discover a mirror that reflects our attitudes and motivations.

It is such an ancient and simple action, yet when we explore sweeping and the many places it is done—inside, outside, at our homes, at another's home, in the streets—we find a sacred and timeless link between the act of sweeping and the work of service. When we think of sharing our love for our fellow humans, rarely does sweeping come to mind, yet if we examine it as an aspect of lovingkindness—as Albanian-born Catholic Mother Teresa suggests through her urging to talk less and speak through taking "a broom and [cleaning] someone's house"—we discover a straightforward and practical way to reach out to humanity.

Part of the beauty of sweeping is its simplicity, and yet the act can illuminate the nature of the person who is doing the sweeping. Dr. Martin Luther King, Jr. suggests that every task should be performed as well "as Michelangelo painted," since our every action is a representation of ourselves, witnessed both by those of this earth and "the hosts of Heaven." By keeping in mind that everything we do extends beyond us—impacting those around us in unimaginable ways—perhaps we will learn to see sweeping as an opportunity for expression.

Just as others witness our actions and behaviors, so too can we find holiness in the most uncomplicated jobs. Examining the motive behind the work we do allows us to find an increased awareness of the effort we put into each task. If we make "drudgery divine"—as Genie is urged to do in the excerpt from *The Mistress of the House*—we can realize that the value of our work is determined by whether our "motive [is] high." Seeing sweeping as a gift, an offering from one person to another, allows us to realize our full ability to manifest the love we feel toward others through our actions.

A "high motive" encourages African American educator and orator Booker T. Washington to experience sweeping as something other than an offering. Washington sees sweeping as opportunity. He writes of it as an external demonstration of his inner worthiness—he wholeheartedly sweeps the room he is instructed to clean in a way that initially makes him proud, only secondarily considering the approval he will receive based on the quality of his work. Washington's mindset demonstrates how our characters are tested in various ways, but it is only after we are fully and genuinely satisfied with what we have accomplished that we can experience the full affect of that work on others.

Sweeping can be sanctified to become a symbol for the self as well as for service. The selections in this section speak to the many discoveries that can be found when we look at sweeping as other than a laborious chore; the writers find power not only in what is swept away, but also in what lingers. By opening our hearts and giving ourselves over to the act, we rise above the physical task and glimpse the world around us with new eyes, eyes that see promise instead of only pain, opportunity in place of stagnation, and action as a solution to the endless problems that echo all around us.

Martin Luther King, Jr. and Johann Wolfgang von Goethe

COMPOSITIONS

If a man is called to be a street sweeper, he should sweep streets even as Michelangelo painted, or Beethoven composed music, or Shakespeare wrote poetry. He should sweep streets so well that all the hosts of Heaven and earth will pause to say, "Here lived a great street sweeper who did his job well."

—MARTIN LUTHER KING, JR.

Let everyone sweep in front of his own door, and the whole world will be clean.

—VON GOETHE

Author Unknown, 1894

MAKING DRUDGERY DIVINE

The table was cleared, the dishes in orderly piles placed in the kitchen sink, the cook stove closed so as only to keep the fire, and then she began at the top of the house. The beds were soon made. "Oh, there!" She meant to have brought the broom and the dust-pan. Now she must make an extra journey to the kitchen closet. Mother never made any extra journeys; she must have her wits about her.

The light had not penetrated into the depths of the closet where the broom hung, but as she took it from the nail, something white fluttered down, and fell at her feet. She picked up the card in surprise, and went to the window to read—

> *Whatsoever ye do, do it heartily, as to the Lord.*
> *Tis this*
> *Makes drudgery divine:*
> *Who sweeps a room as for Thy laws*
> *Makes that and the action fine.*

—in her mother's delicate, distinct hand. The light broke all over Genie's face. Oh, how nice it was! She read it over again, and ran up the stairs.

Every room in use was carefully swept. There was no dust left in the corners or under the beds. "Sweeps a room as for Thy laws," that made it a different thing. It reminded her of the story of the servant girl who said her "religion made her sweep under the mats too." Was any useful employment less honorable than another, if the motive was high?

Shoghi Effendi

"Bahá'u'lláh's Banishment to Iraq"

From such a treasury of precious memories it will suffice my purpose to cite but a single instance, that of one of His ardent lovers, a native of Zavárih, Siyyid Ismá'íl by name, surnamed Dhabíh (the Sacrifice), formerly a noted divine, taciturn, meditative and wholly severed from every earthly tie, whose self-appointed task, on which he prided himself, was to sweep the approaches of the house in which Bahá'u'lláh was dwelling. Unwinding his green turban, the ensign of his holy lineage, from his head, he would, at the hour of dawn, gather up, with infinite patience, the rubble which the footsteps of his Beloved had trodden, would blow the dust from the crannies of the wall adjacent to the door of that house, would collect the sweepings in the folds of his own cloak, and, scorning to cast his burden for the feet of others to tread upon, would carry it as far as the banks of the river and throw it into its waters.

Booker T. Washington

A COMMON THING IN AN UNCOMMON MANNER

As soon as possible after reaching the grounds of the Hampton Institute, I presented myself before the head teacher for an assignment to a class. Having been so long without proper food, a bath, and a change of clothing, I did not, of course, make a very favorable impression upon her, and I could see at once that there were doubts in her mind about the wisdom of admitting me as a student. I felt that I could hardly blame her if she got the idea that I was a worthless loafer or tramp. For some time she did not refuse to admit me, neither did she decide in my favor, and I continued to linger about her, and to impress her in all the ways I could with my worthiness. In the meantime I saw her admitting other students, and that added greatly to my discomfort, for I felt, deep down in my heart, that I could do as well as they, if I could only get a chance to show what was in me.

After some hours had passed, the head teacher said to me: "The adjoining recitation-room needs sweeping. Take the broom and sweep it."

It occurred to me at once that here was my chance. Never did I receive an order with more delight. I knew that I could sweep, for Mrs. Ruffner had thoroughly taught me how to do that when I lived with her.

I swept the recitation-room three times. Then I got a dust-ing cloth and dusted it four times. All the woodwork around the walls, every bench, table, and desk, I went over four times with my dusting-cloth. Besides, every piece of furniture had been moved and every closet and corner in the room had been thoroughly cleaned. I had the feeling that in a large measure my future depended upon the impression I made upon the teacher in the cleaning of that room. When I was through, I reported to the head teacher. She was a "Yan-kee" woman who knew just where to look for dirt. She went into the room and inspected the floor and closets; then she took her handker-chief and rubbed it on the woodwork about the walls, and over the table and benches. When she was unable to find one bit of dirt on the floor, or a particle of dust on any of the furniture, she quietly remarked, "I guess you will do to enter this institution."

I was one of the happiest souls on Earth. The sweeping of that room was my college examination, and never did any youth pass an examination for entrance into Harvard or Yale that gave him more genuine satisfaction. I have passed several examinations since then, but I have always felt that this was the best one I ever passed....

As I have said, I believe that my race will succeed in proportion as it learns to do a common thing in an uncommon manner; learns to do a thing so thoroughly that no one can improve upon what it has done; learns to make its services of indispensable value. This was the spirit that inspired me in my first effort at Hampton, when I was given the opportunity to sweep and dust that schoolroom. In a degree I felt that my whole future life depended upon the thoroughness with which I cleaned that room, and I was determined to do it so well that no one could find any fault with the job.

Gunilla Norris

"SWEEPING"

It's an old friend, this broom.
I like how it is made—
all these bits of brush sewn into one tool.
Together with the handle and my arms,
this becomes a unit
which can move sand and dirt.

I like joining this tool.
The arms move, the handle moves,
the broom head moves,
the dirt moves up and over the threshold.

We are sweeping—a kind of delicate dance
which results in this dirt being outside
now with the other dirt—moved on.
I want to be here with this moving on,
moment to moment, sweeping.

Let my concentration be the handle;
my body's effort, the will;
the broom head like my thoughts
coming together into one willingness—
Moving on, moving on—
Not clinging to anything.

The foyer is tidier and my inner mudroom
more at peace. I am returned to You.
A clean sweep.

Marilynne Robinson

HERE AND NOT ELSEWHERE

I remember Sylvie walking through the house with a scarf tied around her hair, carrying a broom. Yet this was the time that leaves began to gather in the corners. They were leaves that had been through the winter, some of them worn to a net of veins. There were scraps of paper among them, crisp and stained from their mingling in the cold brown liquors of decay and regeneration, and on these scraps there were sometimes words. One read *Powers Meet,* and another, which had been the flap of an envelope, had a penciled message in anonymous hand: *I think of you.* Perhaps Sylvie when she swept took care not to molest them. Perhaps she sensed a Delphic niceness in the scattering of these leaves and paper, here and not elsewhere, thus and not otherwise. She had to have been aware of them because every time a door was opened anywhere in the house there was a sound from all the corners of lifting and alighting. I noticed that the leaves would be lifted up by something that came before the wind, they would tack against some impalpable movement of air several seconds before the wind was heard in the trees.

Mother Teresa

ACTION

There should be less talk; a preaching point is not a meeting point. What do you do then?

Take a broom and clean someone's house. That says enough.

PART FOUR

The Natural Order of Things

When I think about clutter, all of the old truisms bubble up, like, "A place for everything, and everything in its place." Why is that? Rabbi Yitzhak Buxbaum suggests that, "dirt and disorder are usually a manifestation of [our] inner condition." By cleaning up and discarding the physical, tangible debris in our lives, we can rid ourselves of some of the negativity that builds up in our spiritual lives and detracts from our satisfaction with ourselves, each other, and the universe. Different philosophies have various ways of labeling this external disarray. The pages that follow demonstrate how our surroundings genuinely and deeply impact us—emotionally, physically, and spiritually.

Many of us aim to create a sense of well-being and comfort by caring for and organizing the things we can have control over—a sock drawer, a kitchen cabinet, or a toy box. Often, seeking orderliness boils down to taking control of our world when there is so much chaos—greed, evil, hatred—beyond our grasp.

Orderliness can be a way of distinguishing between a house and a home, says African American educator and orator Booker T. Washington. Washington believes a house is a place that is merely inhabited; a home is well-maintained, orderly, and a peaceful example to all who see it. Creating a home is more than maintaining order by simply putting things where they belong; the state of our homes—be they in cheerful disarray or incredibly organized—reflects back on ourselves.

Through orderliness we can choose who we are and who we want to become. It can provide us with a way out of old, seemingly comfortable but, in actuality, limiting habits. Author, professor, and cancer survivor Marc Poirier discovers this escape in his compulsion to organize his routinely cluttered and disheveled life, following his diagnosis of a recurrence of lymphoma. Poirier realized that he hid behind his "ungodly mess," which "meant I did not have to change. I was okay as I was." He didn't need to make decisions and this allowed him to avoid being held accountable for his mistakes. Through sorting, organizing, discarding, and "maintaining external order," Poirier unveils a newfound internal balance and begins to "appreciate [his] life" and live in the moment.

Establishing order and organization is frequently a struggle; as our lives continue to swirl around us despite our efforts to claim control, the task of orderliness can seem insurmountable. Therapist and author Sue Bender felt she was fighting an "endless, losing battle to make order in [her] life." Her solution was to harness time, which forced her to appreciate each passing moment. By limiting the amount of time she takes to tidy a given area, Bender realized she possesses the ability to completely focus on her task, and discover in it the joy and beauty of approaching something intangible within the concrete sense of order she creates in each new—orderly—space.

Seeing within the process of ordering a means to pray or meditate through work can influence how we approach the task of getting organized. By discovering the "essential parts of the journey to wholeness that answers the emptiness in each of us" says Benedictine nun Joan Chittister, we allow ourselves to further realize the sacred in all that we do. It is not a matter of mastering the art of orderliness but realizing the physical and spiritual benefits order yields and working *toward* that. Each step in righting our immediate environments can foster our sense of personal and spiritual well-being—and also, perhaps, relieve some of the world's disorderliness.

Just as what surrounds us affects us internally, so too can we imbue our spiritual joy into each and every task we set our hands to.

French author Henri Bosco exemplifies the cyclical benefit of ordering in his excerpt from *Le Jardin d'Hyacinthe*. When we are able to
experience "little movements of joy" even as we file, sort, or clear
away trash, then will we be more able to "contemplate to [our] heart's
content the supernatural" parts of ourselves that are so frequently
buried beneath the clutter. In those moments, we will work in "the
company of angels."

Lydia Maria Child
and II Kings 20:1

TRUE ECONOMY

The true economy of housekeeping is simply the art of gathering up all the fragments, so that nothing be lost. I mean fragments of *time*, as well as *materials*.

Set thine house in order.

—II Kings 20:1

Booker T. Washington

"A Plain Talk as to Securing Negro Homes"

Only a short time ago near a certain town, I visited the house—I could not call it a home—of a presiding elder, a man who had received considerable education and who spent his time going about over his district preaching to hundreds and thousands of colored people yet the home of this presiding elder was almost a disgrace to him and to his race. The house was not painted or whitewashed, the fence was in the same condition, the yard was full of weeds, there were no walks laid out in the yard, there were no flowers in it; in fact everything on the outside of the house and in the yard presented the most dismal and disappointing appearance....This is not the way to live, and especially is this true of a minister or teacher who is supposed to lead the people, not only by word but by example. Every minister and teacher should [make] his house, his yard and his garden a model for the people whom he attempts to teach and lead. I confess that I have no respect or confidence in the preaching of a minister whose home is in the condition of the one I have described.

Chogyam Trungpa
Rinpoche

"HOW TO INVOKE MAGIC"

[I]nvoking the external *drala* principle is connected with organizing your environment so that it becomes a sacred space. This begins with the organization of your personal, household environment, and beyond that, it can include much larger environments, such as a city or even an entire country.

Marc Poirier

"CLUTTER AND THE MATTER OF LIFE AND DEATH"

When I began to get sick with a recurrence of lymphoma, I prepared for a difficult four or five months of intensive treatment and recovery. Much of this fell into place. My aunt and sister each agreed to stay with me for a month or more, with friends watching over me at other times. Disability insurance fortunately meant finances would not be an issue. I had worked with Zen and other Buddhist traditions for years, and they helped me to find some objectivity and equanimity about my situation. I was working out, so my body was more or less prepared for an ordeal.

But one thing took me totally by surprise. I found myself experiencing unfamiliar and desperate urges to clean my house. I would feel compelled to go through closets and bureaus, sorting and throwing out clothes, arranging and polishing the shoes. I reorganized the kitchen and pantry and threw stuff away. I got rid of all those extra little plastic containers. I cleaned the refrigerator not once but several times. I cleaned out the back of the car and took it to the car wash. I even woke up in the middle of the night once and cleaned all the doorknobs.

This was so unbelievable. I have lived all my life in a world of clutter. I grew up in a cluttered household—clean enough, but with way too much stuff lying around and rarely put away. My father, a professor like me, left books and papers everywhere. When I finished law school and began my first full-time job, I knew I was in the right place, because the two partners who had started the firm both had incredibly messy offices. A framed needlepoint hung on one partner's office wall; it read, "Clutter is the mark of genius."

For me, clutter was comfortable, familiar, safe and easy. My home, office and car simply stayed full, even if I didn't always know just where things were. And as for putting it all in order, more than an hour or two of cleaning up was so boring and, if truth be told, underneath that, stressful. Cleaning up forced me to make decisions I didn't want to make, to permanently dispose of things, acknowledge mistakes, say goodbye to roads not taken. In contrast, clutter affirmed my life, messy as it was, just as it was. Clutter meant I did not have to change. I was okay as I was.

So why, at a time of truly limited energy and health crisis, would I find cleanliness and order so important? And not in any rational, thought-through way—the impulse to clean bubbled up directly from deep within my psyche and overrode my normal habits.

The part I could most easily understand was that decluttering and cleaning made room for others. I expected to have relatives and friends staying in my house and taking care of me, and they deserved to have a clean bedroom and a usable kitchen. In fact, I needed them to feel comfortable in my home even if I had to change my ways to do it.

Cleaning up also seemed to be a bigger version of the old admonition always to wear clean underwear in case you get hit by a car and have to go to the hospital. You don't want the doctor to see you wearing dirty underwear. I didn't want to get sick and die and leave others to deal with all my clutter. My father and brother had both died suddenly, leaving houses, garages and cars full of stuff. It was so inconsiderate. I didn't want to do that to my family and friends.

Creating and maintaining spatial order also seemed to have a deeper significance. My medical treatment involved a total of about seven weeks in the hospital. I always set up a small Buddhist shrine in one corner of my hospital room. I was incredibly protective of that small and orderly sacred space. Nurses would see it as flat space and set down medical supplies or equipment. I would immediately ask them to remove it. The altar's space was inviolable. And I also found myself focused enough to do a series of chants and meditations regularly in the morning and throughout the day. Illness somehow empowered me to impose a temporal order, as well as a spatial order, on my life.

It was strange to me how much I found all this order comforting and nourishing. Undeniably, it had a spiritually uplifting quality. By paring down and organizing the objects in my life, I was discovering something about simple and utilitarian living and ownership, without grandiose purpose or hanging on. I found myself expressing through de-cluttering some kind of faith in the wellbeing of the circumstances of my life, despite my ill health. It was, perhaps, the same impulse that lies behind Zen and Shaker aesthetics.

At some point, I recalled something I had encountered years before, in the teachings of Chogyam Trungpa on *drala*. *Drala* is a Tibetan word. It means something like order. As related in *Shambhala: The Sacred Space of the Warrior*, *drala* includes external, internal and secret aspects. External *drala* as I understood it meant the order of one's things and living situation. I hated this idea. Simply hated it. I refused to believe that putting my clothes away and making my bed had anything to do with spiritual health or truth. Having to keep things in order was distracting, time-consuming, arbitrary, uncreative and rigid. Perhaps worst, it was mean. It seemed the misconceived imposition of some cruel old grandmother figure, who insisted on hovering and judging, making unnecessary upsets and ukases about a messy floor or a spot on a shirt.

Now, in my illness, maintaining external order took on a different character altogether. It became affirming, not mean and distracting. Freed by my illness from any pretense of being a big shot in my work or my hobbies or anywhere else, I was able to take the time to take care of myself. Miraculously, I knew what to do. I and the objects in my life were mostly in accord about what stayed and what went, and what belonged where. Cleaning up became an ongoing affirmation of my own sense of belonging, and of the essential goodness of my life moment by moment, even without purpose or goal. I did not see it particularly as a talismanic magic that would keep me from dying, but as an affirmation that this day and this particular space were fundamentally okay. Through maintaining external order, I could appreciate my life.

I wish I could say that I was thoroughly transformed by my experience while I was sick. But I was not. Old habits die hard. As I got well again, I returned to work. I began to move in the direction of reproducing my old schedule of friends and activities. And with all this activity, the familiar clutter has started to return. Papers are creeping back into the corners of my living room and office. My refrigerator is not cleaned as frequently. (Really, who has the time?) I am noticing that my habitual clutter has other aspects—overwork, over-commitment and overweight. I rush around, feeling there is not enough time. Feeling there is not enough satisfaction, I overeat. We are all creatures of habit, and as I get well my old bad habits are returning.

But I know something about clutter and order that I did not know before, and that is a vital difference. I can no longer be so self-righteous or complacent about disorder. If the habits have not changed all by themselves, my awareness of their sources and consequences has, at least a little bit. Before, insisting on order seemed rigid, dictatorial and a waste of time. Clutter seemed to preserve the possibility of freedom and creativity (as my boss's needlepoint said) and to conserve energy for much more important things (than managing one's life!). Now, clutter presents a threat. It feels clogging and suffocating, the opposite of supportive. The possibility of a de-cluttered and orderly space and life is not only nourishing, but it alone supports the energy and freedom to move on and grow anew.

I am working to be as conscious as I can of how I put order and disorder into my life. I am trying to notice what I do, and seeking to create and appreciate all the little bits of spaciousness and order in my surroundings throughout my day. And actually, the fact that we are creatures of habit—nothing at all but habits, in fact—is good news as well as bad. For our habits, though they may be very deep, are not altogether inevitable. With attention to details and over much time, major shifts can be accomplished.

But this is work! Ongoing work, demanding as much attention as I can give it. Where does this little piece belong, this paper, this bite of food, this minute, this emotion, this thought? How can I offer them up, not as some ungodly mess, but as an orderly and aesthetic expression of the well-being of my life? It is not clear whether my cancer will recur yet again. But whatever the future may hold for my health, this is the direction of my practice.

Yitzhak Buxbaum

"KAVVANAH FOR CLEANING"

Cleaning one's house or washing the dishes and so on can and should be a meditative activity.

The late Rabbi Avraham Aharonowitz, an Israeli Boyaner hasid and a tzaddik [righteous man] in his own right, performed every action with intention, and his every daily deed was a divine service. For example, he himself used to take out and empty the garbage can, although he was a great tzaddik and many people would have been happy to do it for him! But he insisted on doing it himself. And, when he took out the garbage, he did it with kavvanah and attention. He explained that removing garbage and dirt from the house is like expelling the Other Side [negativity and evil] from a person's dwelling, because the negative forces [hitzonim] "draw their sustenance" from waste and leftovers.

The holy books explain that because dirt and uncleanness are the dwelling place of the Other Side, removing garbage is like expelling negative forces.

One needn't use the kabbalistic vocabulary of the "Other Side" and "negative forces" to apply this insight and teaching. If you allow your dwelling to be untidy and unclean, it is because the negative forces of laziness and depression are asserting themselves in your life. The dirt and disorder are usually an external manifestation of your inner condition. When you realize this, you can be inspired to repair your spiritual condition and to clean. As you clean, or make your bed, etc., you can occasionally think or utter such words as: "God, I'm cleaning and making order in my dwelling so that I can be spiritually clean and put my life in order to be close to You!"

Joan Chittister

"THE TOOLS AND GOODS OF THE MONASTERY"

The goods of the monastery, that is, its tools, cloth-
ing and anything else, should be entrusted to mem-
bers whom the prioress or abbot appoints and in
whose manner of life they have confidence. The
abbot or prioress will, as they see fit, issue to them
the various articles to be cared for and collected after
use. The prioress and abbot will maintain a list of
these, so that when the members succeed one
another in their assigned tasks, they may be aware of
what they hand out and what they receive back.

Whoever fails to keep the things belonging to
the monastery clean or treats them carelessly should
be reproved. If they do not amend, let them be sub-
jected to discipline of the rule.

To those who think for a moment that the spiritual life is an excuse
to ignore the things of the world, to go through time suspended
above the mundane, to lurch from place to place with a balmy head
and a saccharine smile on the face, let this chapter be fair warning.

Benedictine spirituality is as much about good order, wise management, and housecleaning as it is about the meditative and the immaterial dimensions of life. Benedictine spirituality sees the care of the earth and the integration of prayer and work, body and soul, as essential parts of the journey to wholeness that answers the emptiness in each of us.

Sue Bender

"ONE HOUR SORTING"

I first read the words "creative ordering" in *She*, a book by Robert Johnson. I smiled, delighted. Adding the word *creative* to something I find difficult—my endless, losing battle to make order in my life—allowed for new possibilities.

I came up with a plan, made a contract with myself that seemed sensible and doable. I would spend one hour a day sorting. It didn't matter which room, drawer, cabinet, closet, or file I picked. One hour. The only rule was that while I was doing whatever I'd chosen to do, I would not spend any good energy noticing how many hours, months, years it might take to get all the other projects finished.

The first day I tackled all the jars, prescriptions, razors, perfume, and shampoo in the cabinet under the bathroom sink. The next day four bookshelves in the bedroom were the focus of my attention. Some books were put in a pile to be given away, the rest sorted into categories.

I was surprised by how pleasurable these small tasks were. They were of manageable size. Manageable and doable.

Having a limited time frame, and without rushing, I was able to approach each job with focused attention. Filling and emptying a big straw wastebasket created a rhythm that was satisfying. That one hour, no matter what else I had chosen to do that day, was as sweet and satisfying as anything I could have imagined doing.

Henri Bosco

In the Company of Angels

[W]hen she washed a sheet or a tablecloth, when she polished a brass candlestick, little movements of joy mounted from the depths of her heart, enlivening her household tasks. She did not wait to finish these tasks before withdrawing into herself, where she could contemplate to her heart's content the supernatural images that dwelt there. Indeed, figures from this land appeared to her familiarly, however commonplace the work she was doing, and without in the least seeming to dream, she washed, dusted and swept in the company of angels.

PART FIVE

*H*ousework

If, as Freud wrote, "Love and work are the cornerstones of our humanness," then perhaps love and housework are the cornerstones of our families—a description that can include our communities, congregations, *sanghas*, and even strangers. This is not to say that we always experience bliss in cleaning, but when we undertake it as an act of love and generosity, the processes that are part of housework can be transcendent. In this section, housework is discovered or rediscovered, ritualized or done on the fly, and is often seen as a gift given to loved ones.

Most of us approach housework with the same complexity, depth, and, oftentimes, perplexing feelings we encounter in many aspects of our lives: Just what is the point? In "The Idea of Housework" American poet Dorianne Laux poses a question that is answered by several other writers: "Why should the things of the world shine so?" In a tone that rings both with frustration at the unreturned milk jugs that are piling up and the longing to "rub the windows with vinegar," to see the "true colors" of the trees, Laux speaks honestly about feeling overwhelmed while she reminds herself—and us—that nature's beauty lingers just outside, making cleaning the windows not futile and pointless but, rather, a practice that allows us to embrace the world's offerings of splendor.

There is a process of strength and hope we can uncover within the act of housework. As Louisa May Alcott illustrates, in the urge to clean house we also find a sense of work and duty that motivates us to scrub away the dirt from our hearts, just as we scrub the grime from our clothes.

Alcott also demonstrates that there is room for dreaming and experiencing emotions that might get buried or forgotten—"Head, you may think, Heart, you may feel,"—as we perform our necessary, daily tasks. We can find an opportunity for a new, refreshed sense of self, a cleansing of the "stains of the week" while we perform the duties involved in cleaning house. Through our purposeful hands we can experience solace, comfort, hope, and joy.

Indian spiritual leader Mahatma Gandhi also presents us with the spiritual benefits we can realize in cleaning house. Transcending Alcott's discovery of hope and joy in each task, Gandhi explains how the most unsavory work, "even cleaning of latrines," when done in a "religious spirit" becomes a compassionate gesture that can con-tribute to healing our world and our selves. Our attitudes, therefore, shape each task we approach in our lives; the state of our minds and hearts determines the quality of our experiences at those moments of washing, cleaning, sweeping, and the other housekeeping jobs we perform each day.

It is easy to view our everyday duties as pointless drudgery, as moments in time that must be rushed through and not appreciated. How would our perspectives change if we saw a link between our daily chores and the love we feel for those we share our spaces with?

Despite assumptions rooted in her feminist ideals, Jeannette Batz shows us that in "the chores [she had] branded oppressive and mundane" we can explore elements of the "creative and profound, bringing us closer to the earth, to each other and to God." In per-forming "routine tasks" Batz helps us find "a patient, peaceful mode" where we can "[turn] off the rational brain and [sharpen] the senses," exposing us to endless possibilities in the mundane, not the least of which are the gestures of love and gratitude we offer to our friends and families.

Giving of ourselves through cleaning our homes can be a way for us to get closer to our partners, children, loved ones, as well as the Divine. Through a dust cloth that gives "warmth to everything it touches," a piece of polished furniture can symbolize our efforts to take care of our households, including, and most importantly, the people in them. As French philosopher Gaston Bachelard succinctly and beautifully shows us, by taking care of the objects around us, we, in turn, take care of ourselves. By doing so, we transform housework from plain labor, to a labor of love.

Louise Rafkin exemplifies this concept on a much larger scale as she explores the benefits of giving back to the world at large through our personal efforts when she joins a Japanese cleaning commune. As she rakes leaves and scrubs toilets for strangers, Rafkin reflects on how easily we become mired in the truly meaningless things: "The complications of my life—what to do or be, where to live—fell away against the backdrop of this selfless community." Many of us define ourselves by those things that "fell away" from Rafkin as she cleaned. Through hard work and developing self-awareness, Rafkin illustrates how housework can foster within each of us the cleansing power of responsibility and cultivate ways we can utilize our every action for both personal and global betterment.

Unlike a prepared meal, housework is never quite finished, as Quaker author Jessamyn West points out as she contrasts cooking with cleaning and shows how "putting a room to rights" does for her "soul what prayer does for others." In this continuity, the ever-presence of our efforts, we can find a sense of welcome and comfort. We live on in each gesture of housework, each swath of the mop, broom, or vacuum—each act becomes a prayer that, when completed, is answered.

Dorianne Laux

"THE IDEA OF HOUSEWORK"

What good does it do anyone
to have a drawer full of clean knives,
the tines of tiny pitchforks
gleaming in plastic bins, your face
reflected eight times over
in the oval bowls of spoons?
What does it matter that the bathmat's
scrubbed free of mold, the doormat
swept clear of leaves, the screen door
picked clean of bees' wings, wasps'
dumbstruck bodies, the thoraxes
of flies and moths, high corners
broomed of spider webs, flowered
sheets folded and sealed in drawers,
blankets shaken so sleep's duff and fuzz,
dead skin flakes, lost strands of hair
flicker down on the cut grass?
Who cares if breadcrumbs collect
on the countertop, if photographs
of the ones you love go gray with dust,

if milk jugs pile up, unreturned,
on the back porch near the old dog's dish
encrusted with puppy chow?
Oh to rub the windows with vinegar,
the trees behind them revealing
their true colors. Oh the bleachy,
waxy, soapy, perfume of spring.
Why should the things of the world
shine so? Tell me if you know.

Louisa May Alcott

"A SONG FROM THE SUDS"

Queen of my tub, I merrily sing,
While the white foam rises high,
And sturdily wash and rinse and wring,
And fasten the clothes to dry.
Then out in the free fresh air they swing,
Under the sunny sky.

I wish we could wash from our hearts and souls
The stains of the week away,
And let water and air by their magic make
Ourselves as pure as they.
Then on the earth there would be indeed,
A glorious washing day!

Along the path of a useful life,
Will heartsease ever bloom.
The busy mind has no time to think
Of sorrow or care or gloom.
And anxious thoughts may be swept away,
As we bravely wield a broom.

I am glad a task to me is given,
To labor at day by day,
For it brings me health and strength and hope,
And I cheerfully learn to say,
"Head, you may think, Heart, you may feel,
But, Hand, you shall work alway!"

Mahatma Gandhi

TRUE SPIRIT

A *Dharma* [principle or law that orders the universe] which does not serve practical needs is no *Dharma*, it is *Adharma*. Even cleaning of latrines should be done in a religious spirit. A man of such spirit will ask himself, as he does the work, why there should be so much foul smell. We should realize that we are full of evil desires. The excreta of a person, who is suffering from a disease or is full of evil desires, are bound to emit foul smell. Another person who does not do this work in a religious spirit but shirks his duty will remove the contents anyhow, and not clean the bucket; such a man does not do the work as a religious duty. He has no compassion in him, nor discrimination. Thus, *Dharma* is certainly connected with practical life.

Jeannette Batz

"THE JOYS OF HOUSEWORK: LATE HAVE I LOVED IT"

A friend used to joke that if I had seven kids, I'd be stirring gruel with one hand and flipping the pages of Proust with the other. She was right about everything but the order—I'd be flipping the pages, then remembering to stir. Housework fails to interest me. I shirked most of its chores for years, studiously shunning marriage until I found someone who didn't expect me to retrieve and launder his socks.

Then, as irony would have it, I began to enjoy washing his socks. I started collecting 1950s cookbooks and asking older ladies whether mayonnaise really removes white rings from wood tables. Either I was turning into my mother or this realm was more powerful than I'd thought. Banking on the latter, I plotted out a doctoral dissertation and began researching the symbolic and spiritual meanings of housework.

What I learned convinced me that the chores I'd branded oppressive and mundane are creative and profound, bringing us closer to the earth, to each other and to God.

At least, that's true when they're done with love. Freshly laundered sheets tucked with care can symbolize and reinforce family stability, keeping home a haven from a cold, confusing world. The same sheets, stained and crumpled and flung angrily across the bed, can undermine that security. When women learn housework's power to nurture, they learn its dark side, too. In times of fewer worldly options, many wielded that power like a CEO, manipulating husbands and children into submission.

Once I'd acknowledged the spiritual qualities of nurture, I began testing the long-vaunted link between cleanliness and godliness. There may be more to it than I thought: Dirt, after all, symbolizes wildness and change, death and decay. By plunging their arms into murky washtubs, reaching deep into the drain to pull out hunks of hair and slime, and carrying bowls of vomit from the bedside, women have confronted—and triumphed over—life's most intimate chaos.

Interestingly enough, women's bodies have themselves been labeled earthy, dark, messy, irrational, in need of ordering and subjugation. The Victorian paragon of domestic virtue was called "the angel in the house," to this day pornography is termed "filth," and family values are said to require "clean living." Why such a tight relationship between dirt and sex? Because sexual "sins" are sins of embodiment, of stained, rumpled sheets, sweat-sticky flesh and broken boundaries. And it is women who are responsible for controlling them.

Anthropologist Mary Douglas studied the "pollution" concept most cultures use to label what is dirty, tracing it, not to hygiene, but to our fear of ambiguity. By walling out certain conditions and setting up standards of purity, we protect cherished ideas from contradiction. What is unclean represents what is unclear; "dirt is essentially disorder," signaling a life both physically and morally uncontrolled.

She who removes the dirt, by contrast, is imbued with virtue; she aligns herself with higher forces. For centuries, housewives have known this implicitly and used it too well; they've swept to calm a furious temper; tidied to convey disapproval; scrubbed floors to prove their martyrdom.

But they've also done the wash to steal a moment alone for prayer. As monks know well, discipline, when chosen, opens up the soul. And drudgery often taps life's deepest core. One of housework's real gifts, for example, is a sense of time so radically different, it's almost an altered state of consciousness. When I rush through the ironing too frazzled to enter this state, I'm constantly checking the clock, checking the height of the pile, counting the shirts. But when

I enter the iron's rhythm, one motion flows into the next, my mind quiets and I finish before I've even noticed my progress. Routine tasks put us in a patient, peaceful mode, turning off the rational brain and sharpening the senses. That transition leaves us receptive, intuitive, cooperative rather than controlling.

Is it any wonder the most intimate conversations take place in the kitchen, anguish poured out to an aproned back or sputtered over a chopping board? In *Beloved*, Toni Morrison describes another kind of intimacy: "that eternal, private conversation that takes place between women and their tasks." Morrison mentions "the interior sounds a woman makes when she believes she is alone and unobserved at her work: a sth when she misses the needle's eye; a soft moan when she sees another chip in her one good platter ..." Is she merely talking to herself, as husbands and children maintain, or are her words a casual prayer, a report to the Creator on her nutshell of infinity?

I think chores can be a form of prayer. I also think, after reading the heaviest tomes in the divinity library, that elaborate sets of chores—spring cleaning, for example—can be a form of ritual. We're used to thinking of ritual as a stiffly ceremonial event at which one sits, stands and kneels with docility, hoping to please the supernatural. But the strongest rituals reveal the sacredness of the ordinary, using particular actions in particular ways to extract its deeper meanings. I don't want to overstate this. Not every plate of pasta is a ritual sacrifice. But the first meal you make for your future spouse certainly is.

Ritual can be defined broadly—as just about every expressive human act—or narrowly, as what happens on a marble altar. But in the middle, where sacred and secular meet, ritual experts look for three qualities: formality, fixity and repetition. If you doubt their presence in the domestic sphere, try skipping the laundry for a few weeks. Or watch what happens when another family member volunteers—and does it differently.

Over years of living, a family's housework takes on definite shapes. There are rites of purification: the dishes, the laundry, the dusting and polishing. There are rites of passage: We cross the boundaries of the home with groceries and garbage. We make home a refuge, then sweep a threshold to the outside world. There are rites of transformation (grinding grain and baking bread, changing grain into food, which would then become flesh, was a religious ritual even in the Paleolithic era).

Finally and most obviously, there are rites of incorporation. Scarfing down our daily bagel, we forget what a powerful transaction the domestic act of sustenance can be. Food gives us strength, continuity, reassurance; it mediates between our vulnerable insides and the outside world, between what is self and what is other. Who fixed the meal and how long it took, who carves, who gets the icing roses, who refuses helpings and why, who scrapes the dishes—all these carry messages of affection or estrangement, power or oppression, contentment or rebellion.

I've not gone so far as spirituality author Thomas Moore, who insists "there are gods of the house" and "to them, a scrub brush is a sacramental object." When you're exhausted after a day in the outside world, a scrub brush is a burdensome collector of hair and dead skin, nothing more. What has changed, for me, is the sense of possibility. I spent my formative years jotting down poetic comments about the theology of paradox. But it never occurred to me to seek spirit in the earthiest, dullest, most repetitive chores I knew.

Louise Rafkin

"A YEN FOR CLEANING"

Who is the foe for whom they attack
With rag a brush and pail?
'Tis dust—but not seen dirt alone:
The heart's dust they assail.
—Rokumangyogan, *"The Army of Peace"*

Some people vacation in Yellowstone, Aruba, or New Orleans. Others go to Bali to lie on white beaches, or to the Himalayas to climb steep mountains. I went to Japan to clean toilets.

I heard about a group of cleaning people in Japan through a friend, who connected me with Sho Ishikawa. Sho, about forty, now lives in Manhattan but had been raised in Japan as a member of a cleaning commune. His parents, who had spent most of their lives in the commune, still live there, and his father is one of the present spiritual leaders.

"It is difficult to imagine cleaning for your whole life," Sho said in the first of several phone conversations. "Growing up, I felt like there was a dark cloud over my head." Sho always knew he would leave the commune, and as soon as he finished school he took off for New York to become a Buddhist monk. After a number of years he left the Zen community, and he's now working in the world of public accounting. Sho became the gatekeeper to my exotic experience. He tried to explain the history of the group.

Ittoen ("One Light" or "One Lamp Garden") is rooted in the spiritual awakening, teachings, and life example of Tenko Nishida (1872-1968). Followers worship Nishida's Oneness of Light philosophy while embracing all spiritualities based in the desire for peace and grounded in the ideal of humble service. (Both Buddha and Christ lived the life of the homeless, I was reminded later, and both washed the feet of others.)

Sho sketched out the life of Tenko-san, as he is referred to by most. In the late 1800s, Tenko-san, a failing land developer, became dissatisfied by the corruption of capitalism. Unwilling to struggle against others for his own survival, he challenged the accepted assumption that one worked in order to live. Tenko-san's awakening occurred after three days of meditation and an insight about the deep, natural bonding between mothers and children. This relationship became the metaphor he used to explain the pure interdependence people could have, both with each other and with "the light," or God. Life was given freely to all and was not something that had to be worked for; work was therefore a way of offering thanksgiving for the gift of life.

Renouncing his family, status, and all possessions, Tenko-san began to serve others. He lived a simple life, scrubbing, mopping, chopping wood, and cleaning what were then rudimentary privies. In return, he was offered food and shelter, even money. Declining all but the bare necessities, giving service became the way he connected with. others. For him, this was enlightenment.

Over the next ten years, Tenko-san attracted followers, and together they lived what he called the life of the "homeless." In 1928, some land outside of Kyoto was donated for the establishment of a community. In the fifties and sixties, the commune had hundreds of members, now, nearly thirty years after Tenko-san's death, only about 150 disciples remain.

I don't think Sho quite knew why I wanted to travel ten thousand miles to scrub toilets with a bunch of people I couldn't even communicate with, and I wasn't quite sure myself. Nevertheless, after a succession of phone calls to Japan, a weeklong visit was arranged that would culminate on the national Day of Labor, a day the entire community went cleaning. Sho's own English teacher, a woman close to seventy who had lived over forty years in the commune, would be my official host.

In preparation for this adventure, I attempted to learn a handful of the many Japanese words for dirty. In addition to the basic word for dirty, *kitanai*, the Japanese language offered a plethora of delightfully onomatopoeic names, each detailing the various kinds and ways things could be soiled. *Gicho-gicho*, dripping with grease, sounded much more disgusting than *gucho-gucho*, messed up or jumbled. My favorite, which I chanted one day while wiping sludge from behind a toilet, was *nuru-nuru*, "slimy." Hopeless at languages, out of my unwieldy mouth the word *shimikomu*, the specific term for ground-in grime, sounded like a whale at an amusement park.

Japan itself was astoundingly clean. Before my week with the cleaners, I spent some time in Tokyo, during which I became thoroughly convinced that I lived in the wrong country. Litter? No. Graffiti? No. Clean people. Clean cars, buses, and streets. Trains were not only spotless, on time, and pleasant smelling, they were carpeted and *upholstered.* (Imagine, if you can, a New York subway carpet after a day of commuters.) People with colds considerately donned face-masks, and poop-scooping for pet dogs was fastidiously executed with tiny shovels and rakes.

But all this cleanliness seemed occasionally to lead to excess. The first time I entered a department store bathroom I was shocked to hear the sound of a flushing toilet as I sat down, *before* I went. I jumped, alarmed at the possibility of being doused from underneath, but there was no whirlpool below, only calm waters. I sat down again, warily, and the phantom flushing resumed.

The next toilet I sat upon sang like a babbling brook. The next, at the contemporary museum, simulated the flow of running tap water. Finally, with difficulty and slightly obscene charades, I learned that many Japanese women were embarrassed by the sound of peeing, and had become accustomed to flushing on the way into the toilet in order to shroud evidence of their bodily functions. This doubled water usage, and officials, fearing shortages, joined engineers in developing the camouflaging toilets. Extreme, yes, but I would graciously accept the trade-off. Sweet-smelling taxis with soft, plush seats, lace doilies on the headrests, and complimentary Kleenex?

I could live with babbling toilets.

By the time I had made my way to the cleaning compound, I had begun to recognize Japan's contradictory nature. Sure, everything was squeaky-clean, yet you can buy dirty underpants, supposedly soiled by genuine schoolgirls, from streetside vending machines. And, though nobody seemed able or willing to speak English, English was absolutely everywhere, albeit oddly configured. "Let's Wedding" announced a bridal shop advertisement, while my brand of coffee was called Blendy. The powdered creamer? Creap. A popular beverage slung the off-putting slogan "Sweat drink!" and the cigarette billboards proclaimed "Today I Smoke." I bought a thermos so I could brew up my own Blendy and Creap (the four-dollar coffee was busting me). The thermos was named Twinkleheart and the tag promised "Fall in love with twinkleheart and she becomes charming happiness for awhile."

I hoped so. I was starting to feel lonely.

The day I was due at Ittoen, I was riddled with apprehension. I still knew little of where I was going or what I'd be doing. At a Kyoto marketplace, a fishmonger asked me where I was staying. I told him and he made gestures as if he were sweeping with a broom. I nodded. He bowed, low, then gathered up sellers from the neighboring stalls. A volley of Japanese nods ensued. Soon I was surrounded by a half-circle of bobbing bowers. One woman gave me a strange green Japanese pastry, and another forced upon me what seemed like a package of dried fish fins. Bowing while shuffling backward, I tripped and nearly landed in a box of spiky sea urchins. The hoopla made me a little nervous. I wondered what kind of cult I was staying with.

I pondered how to spend the few short hours I had left before I needed to board the commuter train that would take me from Kyoto to Ittoen. Meditation at one of Kyoto's famous temples? Quiet contemplation over a cup of green tea?

Hardly. I had read all my books, and suddenly, the thought of a week without reading matter made me panic. Map in hand, I struggled to find a bookstore that sold used English titles. The one shop I found had slim pickings, which forced me to buy several volumes I'd be embarrassed to carry stateside. The most promising one was *Best American Sports Stories*, several years out of date.

I still had two full packs of sugar-free bubble gum I'd brought from home. Provisions intact, I was ready. At the last minute I bought a bag of M&M's at the train station's Let's Kiosk; chocolate might console me if things went badly.

Ittoen was tucked into the hills east of Kyoto; gorgeously kept grounds hugged a mishmash of buildings. A brand-new high-tech semi-high-rise sidled up next to a cluster of traditional Japanese bungalows with thatched roofs and curling corners. I entered the compound feeling renewed confidence. I was quite relieved to find that the place actually existed.

Outside the office, which resembled a typical bank office—faxes, copiers, computers, and phones—I met Sho's teacher, Ayako Isayama, a slight, short-haired woman, in a black karate like *gi*. She politely invited me to follow her to my room, taking off at such a clip that in order to keep up I was forced into a gallop. If I hadn't known her age, I'd have guessed about half. Who said that cleaning aged a person quickly? Even her hands were youthful.

The grounds we passed through were impeccably groomed; maples and mossy rolling hills, a small brook snaking through the center of the many buildings. Several older women, similarly dressed, swept leaves with traditional bamboo brooms and exchanged words with Ayako as we made our way up a forest path. I was introduced as Sho's friend, though I hadn't even met him yet. Nevertheless, I nodded and said, "Good!" each time I was asked, "Sho, good?"

I was taken aback by the largeness of the whole place. From Sho's description, I had imagined a small group of dedicated toilet cleaners living in spartan quarters, buckets and sponges always at hand. Instead, I found a highly organized group that ran what was essentially a small town with its own complicated economy. I would soon learn that the commune supported itself by operating various businesses, including a school for every age group (available to those on "the outside" as well as to members), a printing press, an agricultural program, a theater and performance group, as well as a "theme park" located in a southern province. The park, dedicated to the theme of peace, featured replicas of Easter Island statuettes and a huge "Peace Bell," which, according to Ayako, resonated with a beautifully calming tone.

The group also facilitated training sessions for young factory workers and business people, and as we approached the building in which I was to stay, we encountered a single-file line of *gi*-clad men and women who looked, as they jogged past, to be in their early twenties. Though it was late afternoon and the fall air was crisp and chilling, they wore their flip-flops barefooted, without *tabi*, the split-toed Japanese socks.

"Mr. Donut workers," Ayako explained, "returned from *gvogan*, humble toilet cleaning."

I loved Mr. Donut. Not only was it the only place in Japan that offered free refills on coffee, but the employees would greet each customer with a bow and a phrase something like: "I am your servant. How may I humbly serve you?" Even in the overly polite, ever-gracious world of Japanese commerce (where I had the best Big Mac I've ever had served to me *at my table* by the nicest, cleanest, most pleasant McDonald's worker I have ever met), an average Mr. Donut employee stood head-and-shoulders above the others. I had once passed a Mr. Donut shop just before it opened and saw the whole group of workers, heads bowed, chanting what seemed to be a prayer of thankfulness.

"Four days' training. Humble toilet cleaning, door-to-door service," Ayako explained.

More inquiry revealed that four thousand Mr. Donut workers spent time at Ittoen each year; the training was aimed to promote humility and facilitate group dynamics. For toilet cleaning they were assigned specific houses in nearby towns. And they would seek out a variety of other tasks—washing clothes, babysitting, weeding—wherever they were needed, undertaking such service in the tradition of *takuhatsu*, "roadside service," like the "begging-bowl rounds" practiced by Zen monks, who still visit households to recite religious chants. In the afternoons they worked at Ittoen, gathering wood, clearing fields, and tending the gardens. The last day was spent reflecting on their training.

I marveled as the group passed. It's a stretch for me to imagine a group of American workers, say from Dunkin' Donuts or Burger King, jogging door-to-door, heads bowed, begging to clean toilets.

The building in which I was to stay was old, one of the original ones donated in the thirties by a "Friend of Light," one of the many people who lived elsewhere in Japan and supported the group financially and materially. I settled into my room, a sparse square covered in *tatami* mats and centered with a *kotatsu*—a table with a heater attached underneath. The *kotatsu* was the only furniture in the room, as well as the sole source of heat. By now, late afternoon, the room was already frigid. Ayako switched on the table and demonstrated how to sit tucked under its overhanging blankets. Over the next week I spent many hours squeezing as much of myself as far under the table as possible, bending and twisting like a yogi so that more of me might glean a little warmth.

That night Ayako made dinner in the quiet, dark kitchen in our huge and, except for us, empty dormitory. We chatted in simple English. Ayako's skills were more than adequate; however, our cultural differences made the conversation stilted. I asked if I might be able to clean with the Mr. Donut trainees.

Ayako, considering my request, looked away from me. "Difficult, with no Japanese," she shorthanded. "May not be possible."

She rose and began to wash the dishes. I noticed how dirty the kitchen was, the walls spotted with oil and grease, not at all how I had imagined it would be.

"Saturday," she said. "You clean Saturday, with the group."

It was Monday.

"Morning service at five-thirty," she announced and disappeared behind the sliding door to her room. That first night I set the *kotatsu* over my futon, although it was surely a fire risk. At least my toes wouldn't freeze.

If somewhere there is a record for speed-changing shoes, Ayako, must hold it. As at every Japanese house, each time we entered our building, we left our street shoes at the front door and put on what were essentially bedroom slippers. Slippers came off before entering *tatami* rooms, where socks were the appropriate footwear. Hundreds of these changes happened every day, and Ayako made each as smoothly as if she were an Olympian passing a baton. I stumbled and fumbled, often catching myself with a socked toe on the foyer—a definite no-no. (But because my feet were so often aired, I was pleased to have packed many pairs of clean, fresh-smelling socks.)

At dawn's light I followed Ayako down the dusky corridor of our ancient building, where after my first shoe mishap of the day (still sleepy, I nearly toppled over while making the change), she sped off toward the Spirit Hall. I loped to catch up.

Inside the bare wood hall, both Buddhist and Christian images flanked the altar. At center position was a round window overlooking a view of the forest. Ittoen elders and Mr. Donut people lined up on both sides of the room, settled in *seiza* (kneeling, heels under buttocks) on *tatami* platforms, men on one side and women on the other. I took a seat behind Ayako. Everyone looked more comfortable than me. My ankles and joints started to ache after only a few minutes. With some relief, I noticed, several of the Mr. Donut youngsters began to fidget after a while, though the women in front of me, a few who had to have been over eighty, looked like they could sit folded up origami-wise for hours.

Orchestrated by the current leader—Tenko-san's grandson, a tall, pleasant-looking man of about fifty—the service was both calming and invigorating. We began with a song recounting Ittoen history, and then chanted a semi-obscure Buddhist *sutra*, the gist of which is nonattachment to worldly goods. Morning stretches were performed to the accompaniment of a resounding "*ooommm*," which grew even louder with each repetition.

After the service I raced behind Ayako, back to our place, where she offered me a choice of toilet brush or broom. I chose the brush and was handed a bucket and rag. Both the squat toilet and the two standard toilets were fairly clean, but I did the job well, as I had the notion that I would be judged as a person on the quality of my cleaning. By the end of the week I realized this was stupid, but that first day I practically took the finish off the porcelain and wiped every inch of the wooden stalls and floors.

Ayako set off to mop the entire building and was, of course, finished before me. Experience and a lifetime of cleaning, I told myself consolingly.

Breakfast—miso soup, rice, warmed bits of various vegetables, dried indistinguishable fruit, green tea—seemed at first frighteningly unrelated to my usual fare (coffee and toast), but the warm food in the unheated building actually tasted good. Emulating Ayako, who cites the hundreds starving in Rwanda as one reason she never wastes even a morsel of food, I ate everything on my plate. I marveled at the tastiness of the rice, finding the speckled gruel unusually savory. Upon inspection, however, I discovered tiny fish heads, half the size of a grain of rice. I swallowed deliberately, eyes and all. That week I put many things in my mouth I wished I hadn't. Only by the third day did I find myself seriously daydreaming about pizza.

After breakfast I was free till morning teatime.

"What should I clean?" I asked, as I finished drying the breakfast dishes.

Ayako seemed puzzled by my request and gave me a book about Ittoen, in English, before retreating into her room to tackle stacks of correspondence and translations.

I set upon the kitchen, tackling the counters and scouring the walls with a wire brush and Look!, a Japanese cleanser (which for some reason is pronounced *Rooku*), until I thought they might crumble. Apparently some foreign boarders had recently lived in the building, Ayako reported, and they cooked with gallons of oil and were not into cleaning. Four hours later I had only finished half the area.

"Very nice, much better now," Ayako said, pouring us glasses of thin, sweet yogurt. "Funny American who likes to clean!"

Ayako was the only English speaker in the group, and my Japanese still consisted of that silly dirt vocabulary and a fluent "thank you" and "thank you very much." We ate together, and when we weren't eating in the central dining room (where food was eaten on hardwood floors in *seiza*, in silence, and downed in minutes), she told me stories of her life. Although I thought I had a good understanding of cleaning, it became clear I was completely out of my league.

Ittoen as a community had clearly passed its prime and the dwindling population seemed to portend its eventual demise, but the philosophy—nonattachment and service to others—seemed timeless if not ideal. Members own little personal property, and although each receives a monthly allowance, all other assets are held in trust. Upon joining, all possessions are left behind.

Ayako didn't have much to give up when she joined, at least materially. Born in 1927 into a prosperous family, her parents had lost their land in post-World War II redistribution. A student at a Christian college, Ayako was "terribly depressed and searching." When she discovered Tenko-san's book *The Life of Penitence*, which described his journey from miserable wealthy businessman to humble servant, she immediately knew she had to live that kind of life.

"Either that or die," she explained. "I was weak and did not have the will to live. The world made me very sad."

Unfortunately, Ayako's parents refused to let her join the group, which at that point had already situated itself on the hillside where it now stands. So Ayako spent the next few years teaching English in nearby Kyoto, living by Ittoen principles—serving without remuneration—often sleeping in her schoolroom and visiting the group when possible.

Eventually she joined the community and was immediately disowned by her family. Ayako soon became Tenko-san's official secretary, right-hand disciple, and host to foreign guests, working tirelessly at home and traveling overseas twenty times over the last forty years to share Ittoen's ideals at international religion and peace conferences.

One evening, after a light meal of fish soup, dried figs, and rice, I flipped through the pages of one of Ayako's many scrapbooks while she talked about her life. She spoke of her own spiritual awakening, which literally happened after cleaning a toilet.

"There were lots of spider webs on the ceiling and walls. Mud was piled on the floor. The stool was dirty. I swept the cobwebs and began to scrub. After about thirty minutes the grain of the floor came to be seen and the stool became white. I felt refreshed. Wiping my sweat, I looked behind me and saw the lady of the house chanting Buddha's name, her hands in prayer. It was a meeting of two persons, in prayer and in peace. I went outside and saw a tiny blue flower blooming by the roadside. It was so beautiful! I talked with the blue flower, just like I am talking to you."

I nodded, but never in my toilet-cleaning life had I ever come close to this kind of feeling, or spoken to a flower.

"In my heart I saw a bog tree, with everything in its branches. You, me, air, birds, flowers. I knew everything was related. That was my realization after cleaning that toilet."

I flipped pages, the photos dated back decades. Many pictures documented *roto*, the "life of the homeless," and showed lines of uniformed disciples marching across the countryside or through small Japanese villages. In these, Ayako was often at the head of the group, beside Tenko-san, a man who even in pictures had a powerful, transcendent look. Thin, serious, yet with an open countenance, Tenko-san was usually photographed with a bucket and toilet rag.

"Were you ever scared?" I asked. "Not knowing where'd you end up each night?"

"Once," she said. "In America." She pulled an album from the bottom of the stack. Inside, there were pictures of Ayako with American families, some on a farm and one next to a Washington, D.C., apartment building. And there were newspaper clippings, from the mid-seventies, about a young Japanese "nun" who had volunteered to massage feet at several retirement homes.

"For over one month I did humble service. I spent six dollars," she said. "Two dollars I gave to a church," she added.

I drew out the whole story, beginning with Ayako's middle-of-the-night arrival at New York's JFK airport and the kind black taxi driver who carted her free to Manhattan at the end of his shift. At Penn Station, while waiting for a bus to rural New Jersey, she cleaned toilets and massaged the feet of a homeless woman. It was in New Jersey, during a four-hour trek down a country road, when Ayako had felt afraid. She didn't know where she was going and felt so lonely she almost cried. She passed fields dotted with cows, and most of the farmhouses she saw were uninhabited. When she finally stumbled onto a family home, she explained her mission to the woman of the house simply. "I live in Japan. My work is to help people. May I work for you?" she asked, with her hands in a gesture of prayer.

After a discussion with her husband, this woman welcomed Ayako into their home. Ayako then accompanied her to the grocery store, riding in a car back down the road she had just walked. "I was passing the same cows, thinking I had just been so sad and alone," she told me. "Now I was happy and completely taken care of!"

Ayako stayed at this house almost a week, cleaning, cooking Japanese food, and working in the garden. "They asked me always to pray over their food," she said, translating the Ittoen grace: "True faithfulness consists of doing service for others and ignoring your own interests." This couple arranged for her to spend time with friends, and these folks sent her to others. At each home, she cooked, cleaned, babysat, and by example, spread Tenko-san's philosophy.

One night, while staying in a neighborhood in D.C., she strayed into an iffy part of town. A local beat cop warned her to be careful, but Ayako kept walking.

"I met three black girls who said, 'Chinese lady, you are small but you are charming!' This made me laugh so I wasn't afraid."

Later that evening, when approached by a group of young men, she admits to having felt a little nervous. "I didn't want to meet them, but then one turned around and said 'Nice jacket,'" Ayako paused. "I was very happy then."

Ayako's pureness of spirit was alternately inspiring and defeating. I could not *imagine* going door-to-door in America asking for the "humble service of cleaning toilets." Yet buoyed by her example, I asked several more times about going door-to-door here in Japan. Each time she seemed evasive. Aside from our morning duties, and some translating and writing she requested help with, my time was my own. I felt frustrated; I feared I was going to miss out on the pure Ittoen experience.

But did I need someone to assign me to clean? Couldn't I take the initiative myself, even go into town on my own? I had the outfit, my *gi*-top and my headscarf with its large calligraphed circle of "nothingness." But the thought of knocking on a Japanese door without a translator was daunting. Would they invite me into their toilets? It was doubtful. Still, if I had a pure enough heart?

But did I?

I set about local tasks instead. I tutored English to some teens at the high school and sat in on primary school classes where the newly arrived American teacher tried to teach vocabulary about emotions. Her analogies whizzed completely over the students' heads. "Jealous!" she attempted enthusiastically, with her eyes squinched up. "Like if someone buys the new sweater *you* wanted." Stone faces. In a moneyless community based on nonattachment and peace, I thought she might consider rethinking her lesson.

I de-greased most of the kitchen, and each day spent some time outside sweeping up leaves with a bamboo broom. I felt a little jealous watching the Mr. Donut people jog past, buckets bouncing. I had yet to penetrate the elusive Japanese home.

Occasionally, however, meditating on the task at hand, I did experience something like a moment of cleaning bliss. This feeling was larger and fuller than the at-home experiences of pleasure I've had cleaning for others. Besides, I noted, my at-home work was usually followed by a big fat check and accolades from my clients.

One afternoon I set about clearing the paths of downed maple leaves and fishing mounds of drowned yellow and gold fallen foliage from the fish pond. Watching the carp scatter, I dipped my broom and pulled debris from the pond's rippling surface. The sun worked its way through four layers of woollies, and for the first time that week I warmed up.

I piled leaves all afternoon, transferring them to the wheelbarrow and carting them to the bathhouse where they'd be burned to heat the steamy water for my evening scrub. Each time I returned up the path, several women, also with brooms, waved and bowed. Five or six hours passed gently and without effort. Everything felt right with the world. I thought I might return to Ittoen for a year, or perhaps two! Cleaning and eating well, working without being worried about money, fame, or getting ahead. What else would I do with my life? The well-swept garden looked like a mossy felt carpet rising and falling, while reflections of the billowy clouds floated across the pond.

Then the wind came up.

Within seconds the ground was covered, and I mean *covered*, with leaves. A mass of orange maple leaves shrouded the pond. Carp?

Where? The reversal of my efforts took about thirteen seconds. As the noisy wind decimated all evidence of my work, the sun sunk behind the mountain. Suddenly chilled, I shuddered.

The women down the lane simply withdrew into their houses, bowing to each other on retreat. As the rain of leaves continued, I started to cry.

I wondered: If a forest is swept and no one sees it, was it ever really swept?

I wondered: Would I ever stop trying to achieve Home Ec Student of the Year?

Later, after I pulled myself together in the privacy of my room, I escaped to the nearby town, scuttling down the mountain path in the growing darkness. At the bakery, I bought a chocolate éclair.

At six-thirty A.M. on Saturday about seventy people gathered on the school grounds, each dressed in full Ittoen gear and carrying buckets and brooms. Our destination was in Osaka where, as a group, we'd clean a large Buddhist temple. Ayako, who had been on a similar field trip a week earlier, had been asked to stay home and sweep the garden. I was delivered to Sho's mother, a beautiful gray-haired woman I suspected to be about sixty. She spoke little English. We smiled and nodded while teams were arranged, and buckets and brooms rearranged. My team was made up of seven elderly men and women.

Next to us, a group of teenagers kidded around with each other innocently. One girl I had tutored laughed at the sight of me in my *gi* and official Ittoen head wrap. "*You* clean toilets?" she asked, and her shyer friends giggled behind her.

After Tenko-san's official toilet cleaning poem was recited, we marched out of the compound in a single line, while elders and those staying behind bowed us on our way. With Ittoen flags flying and buckets looped over left arms, we filed down to the nearby town where our buses waited. I followed Sho's mother, actually quite delighted to be a soldier in an army of cleaners!

Arriving in Osaka around eight, we were welcomed by a group of Buddhist priests and a group of lay supporters ready to join us for the day's work. After a brief service and a lot of bowing, each group was given a map and set to task. The teenaged groups headed off to the banks of public toilets, and I gazed longingly in their direction. My team was escorted to a graveled area about the size of a football field and I was given a bamboo broom. I looked around. At first look the ground seemed clean, but closer inspection revealed tiny leaves, cigarette butts, and scraps of litter. My team attacked immediately, each sweeping with abandon and, I soon discovered, great skill.

And it immediately became clear that I lacked this skill. Sweep too hard and the gravel comes up, producing a mound of gravel, leaves, dirt, and trash while leaving bald patches of bare ground. Sweep lightly and nothing moves: both gravel and leaves stay put. I watched as members of my team flicked their brooms expertly with the precise amount of *oomph*. It was as if the bristles of their brooms were programmed to know exactly which particles should be gathered and which left behind. In hopes of getting the "trick," I experimented with left-handed, right-handed, and back-handed techniques. I tried side-to-side and up-and-back. After an hour, I had barely swept a quarter of the area the others had done. The sun came out strong; I was sweating. My head itched.

Temple viewing ranks highly as a national holiday pastime, and soon well-dressed Japanese visitors began to arrive at the temple grounds. I watched for signs: Were we regarded with disgust or skepticism, like a band of chanting Hare Krishnas or over-solicitous Moonies? Some people stopped to watch, and as a foreigner, I was particularly scrutinized. Several people bowed; one woman asked if this was "my job." I told her no, "volunteer." She cocked her head, quizzically. Mostly we were ignored.

Our team covered the grounds like a pack of grazing sheep, and the gravel really did look a whole lot better after we had swept through. As we approached a particularly dirty and trash-laden area, I noticed a group of men sprawled on some stairs outside an abandoned building. After discovering bottles and food in the weeds edging the walkway, I realized these men were homeless. Even at this early hour, most had been drinking. Red-faced and weary, they watched us work. It made me nervous.

As we neared, several men got up and began tidying up the area, throwing trash in the bins and stacking empty bottles. I was amazed. I remembered something Ayako had told me about Tenko-san. In his day, when down-and-outs came to Ittoen, as many did following the war's devastation, each was welcomed and given food and shelter. But after two days, they were required to join work groups or do *roto*. Tenko-san believed handouts would brew resentment and keep people disempowered. Work would reveal a heart of thanksgiving. Here, it seemed obvious that our example had prompted these men to action. One man nodded as I passed.

We continued past the steps until we had covered the whole area. Our leader, a man as slim and firm as a beetle and probably eighty years old, led us tirelessly to an area near a turtle pond. We swept some more. My hands hurt; I suspected blisters were forming on my palms. At times I felt bone-tired, and then a new energy would surprisingly appear. After four hours, I saw other Ittoen groups heading back to the main temple, but our geriatric team seemed intent on working until the last possible moment.

Over the morning I felt like my sweeping was improving, but at quitting time, while working near a small grove of trees that had obviously been used as a toilet, I realized that either Sho's mother or her robust friend had always been working some distance behind me. I looked at the path I'd cleared, and then at the ground they had passed over. Shards of leaves and a tiny confetti of trash spotted my work. Where they had swept, the ground was pristine: a carpet of smooth, gray rock.

They'd swept over every place I'd covered.

Suddenly, I was *really* tired.

We carted our brooms and bags to the main temple, and after a short service with the Buddhists (during which the teens nodded off, miraculously, still seated in *seiza*), we were fed fish-head rice rolls. Before boarding the bus, I stopped to use the bathroom. Twenty or thirty stalls lined up, each with a squat toilet inside. Though they obviously had been recently cleaned, and water still shone on the slick tiled walls, many people, both homeless and visitors to the temple, had already been through. After only several hours of use, they were already dirty. As I exited my stall, a man threw up all over the floor.

On the bus ride back to Ittoen, the skyscrapers of Osaka disappearing behind me, I questioned if I was capable of selfless cleaning. There was certainly no reason I couldn't clean public places, say toilets in the park or even the sidewalks on my street. On my next trip to New York, I could carry a bottle of spray and wipe down subway seats; I could do an entire car in the time it took to travel from Brooklyn to Manhattan. Indeed, there was nothing stopping me from cleaning for some older people I know, one who's quite sick; both would be grateful for the help. For that matter, I could clean my mother's house next time I visited.

But would I? I looked around at the dozing Ittoenites, many clutching the small boxes of caramels that we had been given after lunch. For the first time I noticed how innocent it all seemed. A simple life, but complicated in its implications. Where would you go if you had ambition or a desire to see the world or a mind that thrived, as did Sho's in an arena of challenging numbers?

We marched back up to the compound and were again greeted by those who had stayed behind, each standing silent, hands in prayer. Bowing. Bowing. I returned the bows.

I so much wanted to leave Ittoen, and I wanted to stay. The week's experience had set me face-to-face with my shortcomings and fears. In my cleaning world I got things—money, free time, acknowledgment. Here, cleaning was about giving everything up. The complications of my life—what to do or be, where to live—fell away against the backdrop of this selfless community. Dust to dust? Who really believes it?

My last teatime with Ayako was brief. She offered tangerines, tart and juicy.

"How can others—how can I—live Ittoen principles out there? In America?"

Ayako's eyes were downcast. She carefully separated the sections of her fruit and didn't say anything for what seemed a long time, though this wasn't unusual during our talks. I often felt like I asked too many questions, and the ones I asked seemed obvious when put to her.

"Live a simple life with an affluent spirit."

This was nice, though it seemed pat, like a proverb, valid but in practicality, vapid.

I sipped my tea and flipped again through my favorite photo album, the one with pictures of early Ittoen life. There were several photos of Ayako and Tenko-san cleaning together, which now, after my own cleaning experience, seemed truly beautiful. And another: Ayako with her headscarf tied behind her ears, hands laced together and barely visible over the right shoulder of an aged Tenko-san, steadying himself with a staff, the misty Ittoen hillside in the background.

"Take whatever you wish," Ayako said.

"But these are originals. You must want them?" I asked. "Others must want them?"

Silence. I touched the pictures. I really did want them.

"I'll die soon," Ayako said. "A few will be saved. The rest will burn with my body and go with the ashes of the others, with the ashes of Tenko-san."

She said this matter-of-factly, without any New Age solemnity or the pomp that might have accompanied this kind of bare-bones spiritual announcement. I peeled several photos from the book.

"Take care of everything you have," she added. "Everything given to us is in trust from the Light."

Suddenly, I thought of the place I owned in the Bay Area. Eight years ago, when I had first quit my job and set off for a writers' colony, an adventure I thought might last a year, I had sublet the house. Since then, I had lived in at least seven cities, on several continents, snagged at least a dozen sublets myself, and began my cleaning life. I knew the basement of my house was now crammed full of other people's castoffs, and the neatly tended garden was overgrown. The once bountiful fruit trees were in desperate need of husbandry and no longer producing. A tenant had recently sent me pictures of my bedroom, post-1989 earthquake; a mix of large cracks and hairline fractures criss-crossed the walls.

It was time to clean house.

Gaston Bachelard

DIGNITY

And so, when a poet rubs a piece of furniture—even vicariously—when he puts a little fragrant wax on his table with the woolen cloth that lends warmth to everything it touches, he creates a new object; he increases the object's human dignity; he registers this object officially as a member of the human household.

Jessamyn West

Answered Prayer

The stove does not much tempt me. When I was young, I thought that there was enough time in life for marble cakes and hermits and pigs in blankets. I have begun to doubt it. I make time (this is impossible! What I do is take time) for dusting and scrubbing and gathering flowers. I do this because I live in my eyes and because bending and twisting—what is called big muscle work—exhilarates me. Finger work, which is what cooking requires, I do not care for. To feed a hungry family, yes, but not for pleasure. Julia Child, who puts as much bounce into cooking as is possible while staying in reasonable contact with floor and stove, is still pretty much of a wrist-down operator.

The house cleaner is, compared with the cook, selfish. The cook cooks for others, to give them pleasure. I don't clean house, "put a room to rights," to please others. I do it for myself. It does for my soul what prayer does for others. And it takes so much less faith. House ordering is my prayer, and when I have finished, my prayer is answered. And bending, stooping, scrubbing, purifies my body as prayer doesn't. When it comes to religion, I am by nature a Shaker, not a Quaker.

I do not understand why there are so many more books about cooking than about housekeeping. Is taste more primary than what is visual and tactile? Do the recipes appeal to the technologist in a technological age? The alchemist? Is the recipe a formula? Do you combine this and that, apply heat, and chemistry takes over? There are no formulas for housekeeping. Housekeeping is half interior decorating. And interior decorating is half art. A pinch of this and a gram of that and the oven set at 375 degrees (400 degrees in elevations more than 5,000 feet). We are impressed by such instructions, but art is not achieved by formula. Any fool with a strong back can scrub a floor, but is cooking a science? We can't all be fanatics and produce bombs, but we can all be recipe readers and produce *pâtés* and soufflés and *pots de crème*. That's what the recipe writers tell us, anyway.

The woman who makes a house say welcome *may* do so for the pleasure of family and friends. She does not, however, expect her still life, though it may be slightly askew at the end of the day, to be totally destroyed. But that's what happens to the pot roast and the black bottom pie. That's what they were made for: total destruction. That's why I say the cook is less selfish than the parlor maid. What does the cook have to show for her work? Memories of praise and of sighs of repletion? But she can't live on in her work. She can't be a lark in her own pie and enjoy the scenery after the baking is done. To say nothing of the eating.

PART SIX

Making Home

Home: It's where the heart is. But what does that really mean? When we stop and think about the definition of *home*, our thoughts typically transcend our physical addresses and we conjure up images of comforting places—a favorite cozy reading chair, a child's room where noise and mess and chaos are as much a part of the space as the walls themselves, or the dining room, the setting for cherished events like the last Thanksgiving dinner you had with your father, or a baby's first birthday party. The idea of turning our living space into what feels like home illustrates our desire to instill welcome and peace that can be felt by everyone who enters it.

There is no one best way to infuse that sense of *home* into a space, it is a feeling—an exhale as we walk through the door at the end of the day—that says, "I'm here and now it's safe to be me." This section highlights that exhale, showing us that the ways to breathe those feelings of life and safety into our homes are myriad and limitless—from hanging *National Geographic* pages on the walls of a prison cell, to discovering the sacred in straightening up the living room.

In our homes we are able to express ourselves in unrestricted ways. We can wear, say, and do whatever we want. Our homes offer us rejuvenation and allow us to "let down [our] guard" and remove the masks that we wear out in the world, suggests author and professor Cheryl Mendelson. When we come home and close the door we give ourselves permission to freely be ourselves, without a care to the perceptions of others. We don't worry about judgment; we simply get to *be*. Mendelson's clear differentiation between the self who is out in the world and the self who is at home makes her point that much more provocative: when we are home, we can embrace who we are.

But a sense of home is more than the liberty of private, personal space. Our attitudes play an integral role when it comes to making a home—how we include our spiritual selves within the physical environment. As Buddhist inmate Jarvis Jay Masters learns when he transforms his cell on San Quentin's death row from a filthy cubicle to a sanctuary, claiming a space and making it our own, however dire the circumstances, allows for the opportunity to explore unknown depths of resilience and strength. Masters's entire outlook was affected by turning his jail cell into a "home," just as ours can be when we focus on creating a sacred, hallowed space for ourselves and the ones we love.

The very process of making home can contribute to our sense of security and permanence. If we view tidying up after our families as diminishing work, then that is what it becomes. But if we perceive this task as something sacred that allows us a closeness with the people we love—as author Sarah Ban Breathnach discovers—cleaning up becomes a higher calling. She is not merely picking up after her family, but rather "transforming this room into a safe and serene haven where [we] can come together to enjoy the comfort of each other's company." This "changing the perception" of her task allows her to see the "sacredness in the ordinary." What we experience is empowerment and shared love inherent in the simple, divine task of "homecaring."

Just as the ultimate purpose of making home can change with our perception, the act of cleaning can evolve when done with sacred intention. As we glimpse the beauty of Kate and Becca's cleaning dance in Ursula K. Le Guin's poem, we are reminded that, sometimes, the thing we think we're doing—cleaning—becomes something divine when we focus on it lovingly, peacefully, and wholeheartedly.

Making home often prompts us to take stock of the condition of our inner selves while we survey the landscape we live in. The ramifications of this spiritual cleansing can spill out to the world at large, shaping who we are—or who we can be—as we share ourselves with others in our communities. As American journalist and Catholic social activist Dorothy Day points out, it is in that place between flowers and "mended spaces" that we may be able to reflect on our true purpose on earth.

Echoing this sentiment, Pulitzer Prize–winning poet Gwendolyn Brooks demonstrates that there is more to making home than the immediate gratification of scrubbing floors or drying dishes. When faced with a decision to take a mouse's life, Maud Martha spares it. In that moment, she reflects on the mouse and realizes how it fits into the grand cycle that is all around us. By choosing to share her home with a mouse, Maud Martha may not be making her home cleaner, but she consecrates her living space with her respect for the sanctity of all beings, and creates the enduring lovingkindness at the heart of what we mean by *home*.

Cheryl Mendelson

RESTORATION

The sense of being at home is important to everyone's well-being. If you do not get enough of it, your happiness, resilience, energy, humor, and courage will decrease. It is a complex thing, an amalgam. In part, it is a sense of having special rights, dignities, and entitlements—and these are legal realities, not just emotional states. It includes familiarity, warmth, affection, and a conviction of security. Being at home feels safe; you have a sense of relief whenever you come home and close the door behind you, reduced fear of social and emotional dangers as well as physical ones. When you are home, you can let down your guard and take off your mask. Home is the one place in the world where you are safe from feeling put down or out, unentitled, or unwanted. It's where you belong, or, as the poet said, the place where, when you go there, they have to take you in. Coming home is your major restorative in life.

Attributed to the Buddha
and
Jarvis Jay Masters

Wherever you live is your temple if you treat it like one.
—Attributed to the Buddha

"SANCTUARY"

When I first entered the gates of San Quentin in the winter of 1981, I walked across the upper yard holding a box called a "fish-kit" filled with my prison-issued belongings. I saw the faces of hundreds who had already made the prison their home. I watched them stare at me with piercing eyes, their faces rugged and their beards of different shades—all dressed in prison blue jeans and worn, torn coats—some leaning against the chain fences, cigarettes hanging from their lips, others with dark glasses covering their eyes.

I will never forget when the steel cell door slammed shut behind me. I stood in the darkness trying to fix my eyes and readjust the thoughts that were telling me that this was not home—that this tiny space would not, could not be where I would spend more than a decade of my life. My mind kept saying, "No! Hell no!" I thought again of the many prisoners I had seen moments ago standing on the yard, so old and accustomed to their fates.

I dropped my fish-kit. I spread my arms and found that the palms of my hands touched the walls with ease. I pushed against them with all my might, until I realized how silly it was to think that these thick concrete walls would somehow budge. I groped for the light switch. It was on the back wall, only a few feet above the steel-plated bunk bed. The bed was bolted into the wall like a shelf. It was only two and a half feet wide by six feet long, and only several feet above the gray concrete floor.

My eyes had adjusted to the darkness by the time I turned the lights on. But until now I hadn't seen the swarms of cockroaches clustered about, especially around the combined toilet and sink on the back wall. When the light came on, the roaches scattered, dashing into tiny holes and cracks behind the sink and in the walls, leaving only the very fat and young ones still running scared. I was beyond shock to see so many of these nasty creatures. And although they didn't come near me, I began to feel roaches climbing all over my body. I even imagined them mounting an attack on me when I was asleep.

This was home. For hours I couldn't bear the thought. The roaches, the filth plastered on the walls, the dirt balls collecting on the floor, and the awful smell of urine left in the toilet for God knows how long sickened me nearly to the point of passing out.

To find home in San Quentin I had to summon an unbelievable will to survive. My first step was to flush the toilet. To my surprise I found all I needed to clean my cell in the fish-kit—a towel, face cloth, and a box of state detergent. There was also a bar of state soap, a toothbrush and comb, a small can of powdered toothpaste, a small plastic cup, and two twenty-year-old *National Geographic* magazines, one of them from the month and year of my birth.

It seemed that time was now on my side. I started cleaning vigorously. I began with one wall, then went on to the next, scrubbing them from top to bottom as hard as I could to remove the markings and filth. I didn't stop until I had washed them down to the floor and they were spotless. If I had to sleep in here, this was the least I could do. The cell bars, sink and toilet, and floor got the same treatment. I was especially worried about the toilet. I had heard that prisoners were compelled to wash their faces in their toilets whenever tear gas was shot into the units to break up mass disruptions and the water was turned off. I imagined leaning into this toilet, and I cleaned it to the highest military standards.

I spent hours, sometimes on my hands and knees, washing down every inch of my cell—even the ceiling. When I had finished, I was convinced that I could eat a piece of candy that had dropped onto the floor. The roaches had all drowned or been killed. I blocked off all their hiding places by plugging up the holes and cracks in the walls with wet toilet paper.

After the first days had passed, I decided to decorate my walls with photographs from the *National Geographic* magazines. The landscapes of Malaysia and other parts of the world had enormous beauty, and I pasted photos of them everywhere. These small representations of life helped me to imagine the world beyond prison walls.

Over the years, I collected books and even acquired a television and radio—windows to the outside world. And I pasted many thousands of photographs on the wall. The one that has made my prison home most like a sanctuary to me is a small photograph of a Buddhist saint that a very dear friend sent to me. It has been in the center of my wall for a number of years.

I now begin every day with the practice of meditation, seated on the cold morning floor, cushioned only by my neatly folded blanket. Welcoming the morning light I realize, like seeing through clouds, that home is wherever the heart can be found.

Ursula K. Le Guin

"KATE AND BECCA HOUSECLEANING"

Their bare feet step proud
As arch-necked horses.

Upstairs to downstairs
Their voices call
Like birds on high
And low branches.

Quick as sea winds
They blow through the house
And everything leaps, shakes
And settles back peacefully shining.

Sarah Ban Breathnach

"EVERYDAY EDENS: SPENDING ANOTHER DAY IN PARADISE"

Home is the definition of God.

—Emily Dickinson

"Eden is that old-fashioned House we dwell in every day," Emily Dickinson reminds me as I wander around my living room picking up a purple hair band, colored markers, a young artist's sketchbook, a tennis racket, minutes from last week's city council meeting, a stack of *Beckett's Baseball Card Monthly*, assorted compact discs, one viola, various mail-order catalogs, three days' worth of newspapers, two pairs of shoes, an empty Doritos bag crumpled up next to the couch, and a hairbrush (mine, but probably used by the owner of the purple hair band).

This is Eden?

Poets, it seems, have waxed lyrical about the joys of domesticity for centuries, no doubt because they lived with loving, patient, and nurturing women who created havens of tranquil order in which they could work in peace and comfort.

But did you know that the spinster Emily Dickinson—who rarely left her home after she was thirty-four—was also very domesticated? In fact, her greatest ecstasies were said to be cooking and writing poetry. And since the bulk of her poems were only published after her death in 1886, it was her cooking skills that first won the Belle of Amherst, Massachusetts, her fame for (among other culinary delights) a moist, dense black fruitcake served at afternoon tea and scrumptious parcels of gingerbread lowered in a basket from her second-floor bedroom sanctuary to hungry neighborhood children. Separated from us now by the chasm of more than a century, her contented and self-contained confinement seems to me to be the perfect antidote to late-twentieth-century existence. "I don't go from home unless emergency lends me the hand," she wrote to a friend in 1854, "and then I do it obstinately and draw back if I can."

How I long to draw back, too. To simply sit still for twenty minutes in the backyard basking in the sunshine, watching the birds build their new nests, watching the cats watching the birds, greeting the new blossoms in the garden, and enjoying a fresh cup of tea and Miss Dickinson's letters.

However, before this idyllic reverie can commence, I must clean. I must pick up the debris of our daily life and bring order to this room, for I cannot stand the chaos, clutter, and confusion here for another single moment. There is simply no time for poetic musings.

Or is there?

Perhaps now—of all times—when I am nearly bowed under physically, emotionally, and psychologically by the minutiae of the mundane, is the very moment I need the reverence of poets who bear witness to the sacredness of the ordinary. Then perhaps I shall see not just other people's belongings, but all the beauty, joy, and abundance that literally lies at my feet. If I can be still for a moment and fully enter into the experience of bringing harmony to my home, perhaps I can discover that the poetry of this afternoon is to be found in the perception of my tasks.

For what is the purpose of cleaning this room? Is it simply to pick up trash and dispose of yesterday's newspaper? Or is some inspired action at work here? In the process of transforming this room into a safe and serene haven where my family can come together to enjoy the comfort of each other's company, am I not changing the perception of my work?

We are all given a choice each day. We can react negatively to the demands made on us or we can choose to live abundantly, to transform the negative into the meaningful. Attitude is all. If I do not endow my life and my work with meaning, no one will ever be able to do it for me. If I don't recognize the value of what I am doing here in this living room, certainly no one else can. And if homecaring is not sacred, then forgive me, for I truly have no conception of the Divine.

And so, to lift my spirits and celebrate my choice, I listen to a Bach concerto as I clean. I put on the kettle to make myself a fresh pot of tea. I throw open the windows to catch a spring breeze. Soon my family will return to this lovely and inviting room.

However, before then, I will carve out a precious interlude of time for myself. I will sit for twenty minutes in the backyard basking in the sunshine, with the birds, the cats, and the new blossoms and contemplate the blessing of having spent another day in Paradise.

Dorothy Day

First Job

January

Today it was warmer and we went to the neighboring farm for our milk. It is an old log house with ancient boxwood in front, but all is in bad repair and unpainted. The hills rose in folds on all sides and there was the beauty of yellow fields, green pines and blue sky. But the fences were down, the barns decrepit, all decaying. It is this way everywhere in the country. One old woman and her son are left, the others all gone to the cities. At all the farms they sell their cream and one can buy only skim milk, for ten cents a quart.

People lived far more substantially, far more beautifully once.

I remember [my daughter] Tamar saying before her marriage—"I don't care if we have no food, I am going to have flowers around my house." But paint and mended fences are needed too, and that means money, time and strength.

It is true we have here "no lasting city," no abiding dwellings; it is true we are on pilgrimage, but, as St. Catherine of Sienna said "all the way to Heaven is Heaven for He said 'I am the Way.'" So it is our duty to take the materials God gives and take up our job of co-creator, and do the best we can.

St. Francis' first job was to clean up a church. The family's first job is the home.

Gwendolyn Brooks

"MAUD MARTHA SPARES THE MOUSE"

There. She had it at last. The weeks it had devoted to eluding her, the tricks, the clever hide-and-go-seeks, the routes it had in all sobriety devised, together with the delicious moments it had, undoubtedly, laughed up its sleeve—all to no ultimate avail. She had that mouse.

It shook its little self, as best it could, in the trap. Its bright black eyes contained no appeal—the little creature seemed to understand that there was no hope of mercy from the eternal enemy, no hope of reprieve or postponement—but a fine small dignity. It waited. It looked at Maud Martha.

She wondered what else it was thinking. Perhaps that there was not enough food in its larder. Perhaps that little Betty, a puny child from the start, would not, now, be getting fed. Perhaps that, now, the family's seasonal housecleaning, for lack of expert direction, would be left undone. It might be regretting that young Bobby's education was now at an end. It might be nursing personal regrets. No more the mysterious shadows of the kitchenette, the uncharted twists, the unguessed halls. No more the sweet delights of the chase, the charms of being unsuccessfully hounded, thrown at.

Maud Martha could not bear the little look.

"Go home to your children," she urged. "To your wife or husband." She opened the trap. The mouse vanished.

Suddenly, she was conscious of a new cleanness in her. A wide air walked in her. A life had blundered its way into her power and it had been hers to preserve or destroy. She had not destroyed. In the center of that simple restraint was—creation. She had created a piece of life. It was wonderful.

"Why," she thought, as her height doubled, "why, I'm good! I am good." She ironed her aprons. Her back was straight. Her eyes were mild, and soft with loving kindness.

PART SEVEN

Workspace

Just as taking care of our homes can be a vocation, tending to our workspaces can be an invocation. In thinking about the relationship between clean and holy as it relates to the spaces where we work, we can consider whether the process of cleaning prepares us for work, or if the clean space provides an environment conducive to work being done. In this section, writers approach the answer to this question from different points in the sacred/mundane continuum, and they all find something distinctly divine in the process of sanctifying their workplace.

Exploring the relationship between cleaning and creating offers us the opportunity to witness an intrinsic link between these seemingly unrelated aspects of our lives. We realize that each of our actions flows into the next—there is no beginning or end—and something as simple as an orderly desktop can become an inspiration. American poet Billy Collins advises that, "the more you clean, the more brilliant / your writing will be," emphasizing how deeply our external surroundings can affect our creative and spiritual selves.

It's easy to overlook the value of the preparation for work. When we rush through preliminary tasks, we are not making ourselves completely available to all we can learn in the moment. True preparation comes from clearing a space where we will see "the ingredients we already have in our lives," as Buddhist teachers Bernard Glassman and Rick Fields point out. Those spaces that need to be cleaned may be in our hearts for a relationship, our minds for a challenge, or our countertops for a meal, but regardless of location we are admonished against speeding to the finish. Exercising enough patience and sensitivity to acknowledge the connection between cleaning and creating—as a painter might prepare a canvas—allows us room to more fully express ourselves, and more completely give ourselves over to the work we are doing.

In that surrender of self, we can view our tools and instruments—be they pencils, brooms, or pans—with a fresh perspective. Whether we begin with dusting a desk or, as in Rainer Maria Rilke's case, polishing a piano, we can discover a deeper beauty that arises as a result of our loving attention. When we immerse ourselves in the task of readying our workspaces, we summon the grandeur of empires and the piety of saints, elevating our mindset and our work to the status of something distinctly divine.

The process of cleaning can also give birth to the work itself. Poet Tess Gallagher offers a completely different and honest look at the holy link between cleaning and work as she points out the never-ending cycle of her occupation: "I'll get back / to the poem," she says, even as she recognizes that "for now / there's a shirt" that needs folding. However, when all is said and done, her act of folding laundry has become the poem—her work—optimistically suggesting that there is a way to unite, and find the poetry in, all that we do. Gallagher demonstrates the transformation and blending of the many responsibilities we juggle every day, and offers a source of inspiration as we witness her incorporate her home life into her work life—in her words, we find encouragement to do the same.

Through cleaning and preparing the spaces where we work, we can discover an openness of our hearts and minds as we derive inspiration from the outside in, permeating our spiritual selves. The sense of order encourages us to perform our work more readily, from a place of preparation that lies deep within us.

Billy Collins

"ADVICE TO WRITERS"

Even if it keeps you up all night,
wash down the walls and scrub the floor
of your study before composing a syllable.

Clean the place as if the Pope were on his way.
Spotlessness is the niece of inspiration.

The more you clean, the more brilliant
your writing will be, so do not hesitate to take
to the open fields to scour the undersides
of rocks or swab in the dark forest
upper branches, nests full of eggs.

When you find your way back home
and stow the sponges and brushes under the sink,
you will behold in the light of dawn
the immaculate altar of your desk,
a clean surface in the middle of a clean world.

From a small vase, sparkling blue, lift
a yellow pencil, the sharpest of the bouquet,
and cover the pages with tiny sentences
like long rows of devoted ants
that followed you in from the woods.

Bernard Glassman and
Rick Fields

"Cleaning the Kitchen Is Cleaning the Mind"

Right now, right in front of us, we have everything we need to begin.

Usually, when we want to begin a new project—whether it be a new business or a new relationship or a new life—we're in a hurry. We want to jump right in and do something—anything. But the Zen cook knows that we can't prepare a meal if the kitchen is cluttered with last night's dishes. In order to see the ingredients we already have in our lives, we need to clear a space. "Clean the chopsticks, ladles, and all other utensils," [Zen master] Dogen advises. "Handle them with equal care and awareness, putting everything back where it naturally belongs."

So we always begin by cleaning. Even if the kitchen looks clean, we still have to clean it again each time we want to start a new meal. It's like taking a glass from the cupboard. We wipe it off before giving it to a guest.

The cleaning process itself changes the cook as well as the surroundings and the people who come into those surroundings—whether we're in a Zen meditation hall, a living room, a kitchen, or an office. That is why so much emphasis is placed on cleaning in a Zen monastery. It doesn't matter whether we think anything is dirty or not. We just clean.

The process of cleaning also allows us to discover the ingredients that are already in this space. We begin to see the ingredients we already have. Before we start to reclean the shelves, for instance, we have to take out the jars. In doing so, we see all the jars we have and find that some are empty, some are almost empty, and others are full. We find out what we don't need, what we have too much of, what's been spoiled, and what needs to be thrown away.

Of course cleaning is an ideal that is never satisfied. Therefore, because we can't fully clean, what we have left becomes part of the ingredients of each new meal. Because we can't clean that glass, our new actions are preconditioned by that dirty glass. So we practice to make each new action as clean and unconditioned as possible.

Tenzin Gyatso,
the 14th Dalai Lama

ENGAGE

The environment where you are doing the meditation should be properly cleaned. While cleaning, you should cultivate the motivation that since you are engaged in the task of accumulating great stores of merit by inviting the hosts of buddhas and bodhisattvas to this environment, it is important to have a clean place. You should see that all the external dirt and dust around you is basically a manifestation of the faults and stains within your own mind. You should see that the most important aim is to purge these stains and faults from within your mind. Therefore, as you cleanse the environment, think that you are also purifying your mind. Develop the very strong thought that by cleaning this place you are inviting the host of buddhas and bodhisattvas who are of the most supreme merit field, and that you will subsequently engage in a path that will enable you to purge your mind of the stains of delusions.

Rainer Maria Rilke

PRACTICE

Under my zealous dust cloth, it [the piano] suddenly started to purr mechanically ... and its fine, deep black surface became more and more beautiful. When you've been through this there's little you don't know! ... Politeness tinged with mischief was my reaction to the friendliness of these objects, which seemed happy to be so well treated, so meticulously renovated. And even today, I must confess that while everything about me grew brighter and the immense black surface of my work table, which dominated its surroundings ... became newly aware, somehow, of the size of the room, reflecting it more and more clearly: pale gray and almost square ... well, yes, I felt moved, as though something were happening, something, to tell the truth, which was not purely superficial but immense, and which touched my very soul: I was an emperor washing the feet of the poor, or Saint Bonaventure, washing dishes in his convent.

Virginia Woolf

SPIRIT

At about nine o'clock at night, on every alternate Wednesday, Miss Mary Datchet made the same resolve, that she would never again lend her rooms for any purposes whatsoever. Being, as they were, rather large and conveniently situated in a street mostly dedicated to offices off the Strand, people who wished to meet, either for purposes of enjoyment, or to discuss art, or to reform the State, had a way of suggesting that Mary had better be asked to lend them her rooms. She always met the request with the same frown of well-simulated annoyance, which presently dissolved in a kind of half-humorous, half-surly shrug, as of a large dog tormented by children who shakes his ears. She would lend her room, but only on condition that all the arrangements were made by her. This fortnightly meeting of a society for the free discussion of everything entailed a great deal of moving, and pulling, and ranging of furniture against the wall, and placing of breakable and precious things in safe places. Miss Datchet was quite capable of lifting a kitchen table on her back, if need were, for although well-proportioned and dressed becomingly, she had the appearance of unusual strength and determination.

She was some twenty-five years of age, but looked older because she earned, or intended to earn, her own living, and had already lost the look of the irresponsible spectator, and taken on that of the private in the army of workers. Her gestures seemed to have a certain purpose, the muscles round eyes and lips were set rather firmly, as though the senses had undergone some discipline, and were held ready for a call on them. She had contracted two faint lines between her eyebrows, not from anxiety but from thought, and it was quite evident that all the feminine instincts of pleasing, soothing, and charming were crossed by others in no way peculiar to her sex. For the rest she was brown-eyed, a little clumsy in movement, and suggested country birth and a descent from respectable hard-working ancestors, who had been men of faith and integrity rather than doubters or fanatics.

At the end of a fairly hard day's work it was certainly something of an effort to clear one's room, to pull the mattress off one's bed, and lay it on the floor, to fill a pitcher with cold coffee, and to sweep a long table clear for plates and cups and saucers, with pyramids of little pink biscuits between them; but when these alterations were effected, Mary felt a lightness of spirit come to her, as if she had put off the stout stuff of her working hours and slipped over her entire being some vesture of thin, bright silk. She knelt before the fire and looked out into the room. The light fell softly, but with clear radiance, through shades of yellow and blue paper, and the room, which was set with one or two sofas resembling grassy mounds in their lack of shape, looked unusually large and quiet. Mary was led to think of the heights of a Sussex down, and the swelling green circle of some camp of ancient warriors. The moonlight would be falling there so peacefully now, and she could fancy the rough pathway of silver upon the wrinkled skin of the sea.

"And here we are," she said, half aloud, half satirically, yet with evident pride, "talking about art."

Tess Gallagher

"I Stop Writing the Poem"

I stop writing the poem
to fold the clothes. No matter who lives
or who dies, I'm still a woman.
I'll always have plenty to do.
I bring the arms of his shirt
together. Nothing can stop
our tenderness. I'll get back
to the poem. I'll get back to being
a woman. But for now
there's a shirt, a giant shirt
in my hands, and somewhere a small girl
standing next to her mother
watching to see how it's done.

Kakuzo Okakura

CONSECRATION

[H]owever faded the tearoom and the tea-equipage may seem, every-thing is absolutely clean. Not a particle of dust will be found in the darkest corner, for if any exists the host is not a tea-master. One of the first requisites of a tea-master is the knowledge of how to sweep, clean, and wash, for there is an art in cleaning and dusting. A piece of antique metal work must not be attacked with the unscrupulous zeal of the Dutch housewife. Dripping water from a flower vase need not be wiped away, for it may be suggestive of dew and coolness.

In this connection there is a story of Rikiu which well illustrates the ideas of cleanliness entertained by the tea-masters. Rikiu was watching his son Shoan as he swept and watered the garden path. "Not clean enough," said Rikiu, when Shoan had finished his task, and bade him try again. After a weary hour the son turned to Rikiu: "Father, there is nothing more to be done. The steps have been washed for the third time, the stone lanterns and the trees are well-sprinkled with water, moss and lichens are shining with a fresh ver-dure; not a twig, not a leaf have I left on the ground."

"Young fool," chided the tea-master, "that is not the way a gar-den path should be swept." Saying this, Rikiu stepped into the gar-den, shook a tree and scattered over the garden gold and crimson leaves, scraps of the brocade of autumn! What Rikiu demanded was not cleanliness alone, but the beautiful and the natural also.

... The simplicity of the tearoom and its freedom from vulgarity make it truly a sanctuary from the vexations of the outer world. There, and there alone, one can consecrate himself to undisturbed adoration of the beautiful.

In the sixteenth century the tearoom afforded a welcome respite from labor to the fierce warriors and statesmen engaged in the unification and reconstruction of Japan. In the seventeenth century, after the strict formalism of the Tokugawa rule had been developed, it offered the only opportunity possible for the free communion of artistic spirits. Before a great work of art there was no distinction between daimyo, samurai, and commoner. Nowadays industrialism is making true refinement more and more difficult all the world over. Do we not need the tearoom more than ever?

PART EIGHT

Guests and Holidays

Cleaning and readying for holidays and guests is often the fun of housekeeping and can be as much of an event as the event itself. Beyond tidying the house, setting the table, or even cooking dinner is the promise of something greater. Preparing for guests—be they friends, family, strangers ... even prophets—stirs our spirit of hospitality, encouraging us to share ourselves completely with those we love—and perhaps those we don't yet know.

Hospitality as a sacred practice stems back to the earliest offerings to a divine being. Engaging our own potential for hospitality changes how we clean our homes and prepare our food. As we ready for guests, our attention to detail is sharpened to the slightest disarray. We become aware of our capabilities and our shortcomings; our energies flag only after the final obligations have been fulfilled. As Nathaniel Hawthorne points out, our own expectations are heightened as we envision our homes and taste our food through the experience of our guests. "She watched the fish with as much tender care and minuteness of attention as if ... her own heart were on the gridiron," Hawthorne tells us of Hepzibah preparing breakfast for her guest, "and her immortal happiness were involved in its being done precisely to a turn!"

For many of us, our homes are manifestations of ourselves. Cleaning in anticipation of visitors becomes an expression of our generosity, of our hope that those we invite to share our living spaces will feel comfortable, welcome, and nourished. Amid the hubbub of preparing for the arrival of guests, it becomes easy to lose sight of what is truly important, like actually sharing time with them, and that which is, in the grand scheme of things, less important, like whether *every* particle of dust has been removed from our homes. In a Bible verse from the book of Luke, Jesus admonishes against becoming so absorbed in preparing for our guests that we never actually get to enjoy them once they arrive. The "good part," he mentions, is learning to discern when to stop preparing and start participating.

As the selections in this section illustrate, it is easy for us to slip into perpetual busyness as we ready ourselves to entertain or host a holiday celebration. For many of us, the act of preparing becomes our prayer for perfection. It is when that prayer is tainted with anger and resentment at the tasks we're doing, and we perform them out of obligation rather than the service of hospitality, that our actions become not "the good part," but something considerably less.

Henri Nouwen describes hospitality as "the creation of a free space where the stranger can enter and become a friend instead of an enemy." In preparing our homes for guests, we can, just as the Creek Indians do, welcome the opportunity to transform ourselves as well as our dwellings, to seek renewal and shed the difficulties and struggles of the past. With the holiday as a prompt to spring us into action, we can experience a sense of rebirth, letting go of the stains we are holding in our hearts and minds, and emerging with a willingness to celebrate the grace of hospitality within ourselves that we can then extend to those who visit us—be they human or Divine.

Homer

FEAST

But Euryclea called the maids and said, "Come, wake up; set about sweeping the cloisters and sprinkling them with water to lay the dust; put the covers on the seats; wipe down the tables, some of you, with a wet sponge; clean out the mixing-jugs and the cups, and go for water from the fountain at once; the suitors will be here directly; they will be here early, for it is a feast day."

Nathaniel Hawthorne

GRACE

When Phoebe awoke—which she did with the early twittering of the conjugal couple of robins in the pear-tree—she heard movements below stairs, and, hastening down, found Hepzibah already in the kitchen. She stood by a window, holding a book in close contiguity to her nose, as if with the hope of gaining an olfactory acquaintance with its contents, since her imperfect vision made it not very easy to read them. If any volume could have manifested its essential wisdom in the mode suggested, it would certainly have been the one now in Hepzibah's hand; and the kitchen, in such an event, would forthwith have streamed with the fragrance of venison, turkeys, capons, larded partridges, puddings, cakes, and Christmas pies, in all manner of elaborate mixture and concoction. It was a cookery book, full of innumerable old fashions of English dishes, and illustrated with engravings, which represented the arrangements of the table at such banquets as it might have befitted a nobleman to give in the great hall of his castle. And, amid these rich and potent devices of the culinary art (not one of which, probably, had been tested, within the memory of any man's grandfather), poor Hepzibah was seeking for some nimble little tidbit, which, with what skill she had, and such materials as were at hand, she might toss up for breakfast.

Soon, with a deep sigh, she put aside the savory volume, and inquired of Phoebe whether old Speckle, as she called one of the hens, had laid an egg the preceding day. Phoebe ran to see, but returned without the expected treasure in her hand. At that instant, however, the blast of a fish-dealer's conch was heard, announcing his approach along the street. With energetic raps at the shop-window, Hepzibah summoned the man in, and made purchase of what he warranted as the finest mackerel in his cart, and as fat a one as ever he felt with his finger so early in the season. Requesting Phoebe to roast some coffee— which she casually observed was the real mocha, and so long kept that each of the small berries ought to be worth its weight in gold—the maiden lady heaped fuel into the vast receptacle of the ancient fireplace in such quantity as soon to drive the lingering dusk out of the kitchen. The country-girl, willing to give her utmost assistance, proposed to make an Indian cake, after her mother's peculiar method, of easy manufacture, and which she could vouch for as possessing a richness, and, if rightly prepared, a delicacy, unequalled by any other mode of breakfast-cake. Hepzibah gladly assenting, the kitchen was soon the scene of savory preparation. Perchance, amid their proper element of smoke, which eddied forth from the ill-constructed chimney, the ghosts of departed cook-maids looked wonderingly on, or peeped down the great breadth of the flue, despising the simplicity of the projected meal, yet ineffectually pining to thrust their shadowy hands into each inchoate dish. The half-starved rats, at any rate, stole visibly out of their hiding-places, and sat on their hind-legs, snuffing the fumy atmosphere, and wistfully awaiting an opportunity to nibble.

Hepzibah had no natural turn for cookery, and, to say the truth, had fairly incurred her present meagerness by often choosing to go without her dinner rather than be attendant on the rotation of the spit, or ebullition of the pot. Her zeal over the fire, therefore, was quite an heroic test of sentiment. It was touching, and positively worthy of tears (if Phoebe, the only spectator, except the rats and ghosts aforesaid, had not been better employed than in shedding them), to see her rake out a bed of fresh and glowing coals, and proceed to broil the mackerel. Her usually pale cheeks were all ablaze with heat and hurry. She watched the fish with as much tender care and minuteness of attention as if—we know not how to express it otherwise—as if her own heart were on the gridiron, and her immortal happiness were involved in its being done precisely to a turn!

Life, within doors, has few pleasanter prospects than a neatly arranged and well-provisioned breakfast table. We come to it freshly, in the dewy youth of the day, and when our spiritual and sensual elements are in better accord than at a later period; so that the material delights of the morning meal are capable of being fully enjoyed, without any very grievous reproaches, whether gastric or conscientious, for yielding even a trifle overmuch to the animal department of our nature. The thoughts, too, that run around the ring of familiar guests have a piquancy and mirthfulness, and oftentimes a vivid truth, which more rarely find their way into the elaborate intercourse of dinner. Hepzibah's small and ancient table, supported on its slender and graceful legs, and covered with a cloth of the richest damask, looked worthy to be the scene and center of one of the cheerfulest of parties. The vapor of the broiled fish arose like incense from the shrine of a barbarian idol, while the fragrance of the mocha might have gratified the nostrils of a tutelary Lar, or whatever power has scope over a modern breakfast table.

Phoebe's Indian cakes were the sweetest offering of all—in their hue befitting the rustic altars of the innocent and golden age—or, so brightly yellow were they, resembling some of the bread which was changed to glistening gold when Midas tried to eat it. The butter must not be forgotten—butter which Phoebe herself had churned, in her own rural home, and brought it to her cousin as a propitiatory gift—smelling of clover blossoms, and diffusing the charm of pastoral scenery through the dark-paneled parlor. All this, with the quaint gorgeousness of the old china cups and saucers, and the crested spoons, and a silver cream jug (Hepzibah's only other article of plate, and shaped like the rudest porringer), set out a board at which the stateliest of old Colonel Pyncheon's guests need not have scorned to take his place. But the Puritan's face scowled down out of the picture, as if nothing on the table pleased his appetite.

By way of contributing what grace she could, Phoebe gathered some roses and a few other flowers, possessing either scent or beauty, and arranged them in a glass pitcher, which, having long ago lost its handle, was so much the fitter for a flower vase.

The early sunshine—as fresh as that which peeped into Eve's bower while she and Adam sat at breakfast there—came twinkling through the branches of the pear-tree, and fell quite across the table.

All was now ready. There were chairs and plates for three. A chair and plate for Hepzibah—the same for Phoebe—but what other guest did her cousin look for?

Luke 10:38–41

THE GOOD PART

Now it came to pass, as they went, that he entered into a certain village: and a certain woman named Martha received him into her house. And she had a sister called Mary, which also sat at Jesus' feet, and heard his word. But Martha was cumbered about much serving, and came to him, and said, "Lord, dost thou not care that my sister hath left me to serve alone? Bid her therefore that she help me."

And Jesus answered and said unto her, "Martha, Martha, thou art careful and troubled about many things: But one thing is needful: and Mary hath chosen that good part, which shall not be taken away from her."

Amiya Corbin

"MARTHA"

"Come unto me,... and I Will give you rest.... " With the automatic persistence of a mantra, these words of her Lord repeated themselves in Martha's brain as she laid herself down to rest one hot afternoon. She felt more tired than usual; there were so many extra things to be done whenever the Master came to visit them, and He was coming that very evening. Though physically tired, Martha felt none of the nervous exhaustion which had usually accompanied her former preparations, and as she lay there, she recalled again, as she so often did, that never-to-be-forgotten day when Jesus had taught her the great secret of service.

What a day that had been! It seemed that everything had gone wrong from the very moment she got up that morning. There was yet much to be done, and she still felt nervous and tired from the previous day's activities, and, to make matters worse, Mary was nowhere to be found. Not that she was ever much help nowadays. Ever since their first meeting with the Master, she had changed. She had always been something of a dreamer, and, since the coming of Jesus, she would spend hours alone in her room or in the garden. Martha knew she was always thinking of Him, and the things He had taught her, and it was all right with her; she sometimes wished that she, too, had time to daydream or "meditate" as Mary called it. But everybody couldn't be dreamers. There were things to be done; household duties didn't just drop away, that she knew only too well; but that she should go off completely at such a time was too much for Martha. She became furious, and it did nothing to lessen her annoyance when later Mary arrived with the Master and His friends, whom she had gone out to meet.

Martha recalled how curtly she had welcomed the guests, and how angry she had felt toward Mary as she returned to the kitchen and the cooking. She had been sure that Mary would at least help her serve the meal. Looking back over the scene it was difficult for Martha now to understand how she could have allowed herself to get so upset. But upset she had been! She could have shaken her sister, but instead she had made that ghastly mistake! A chill ran over her as she recalled that most dreadful scene. Why could not Mary have used some initiative, why could she not have felt Martha's extremity, and at least have offered to help? How much pain it might have saved! Or so Martha thought. But when, instead, poor Martha lost her last ounce of control and burst in upon them, there was Mary sitting at the feet of Jesus, looking up into His face, and listening to His words with rapt attention! And then the reproach that followed her demand for help! "Martha, Martha, thou art careful and troubled about many things: but one thing is needful: and Mary hath chosen that good part...." Poor Martha! Stunned and crushed, she returned to her kitchen. She wondered vaguely what Mary thought about it all. Did she understand what He meant by the "good part?" She did not blame her sister; rather she felt that somehow she herself was at fault, but how? In silence she served her guests, only waiting till she could steal away to the solitude of her own room.

All that afternoon the question haunted her: what was that one needful thing, what was that "good part?" In what way was Mary's part better than hers? In what way were they different? She tried to recall something Jesus might sometime have said which would answer the question for her, but in vain. She realized sadly that she had always been too busy to find much time to sit at His feet like Mary did, and listen to His teachings. She realized that she was with Him only at mealtimes, and these times were always occasions of festivity. Perhaps, after all, in her anxiety to serve Him, she had actually neglected Him! But He came so seldom, His life was so lonely, His comforts so few, that she had always felt that no effort was too great, no service too small, if only she could give Him even a little happiness and comfort. Didn't He know that? Didn't He know why she had been angry at Mary? Surely He must know; and He must also know the agony of remorse that followed her outburst.

She did not see Him again that day until she went to bid Him goodnight as He sat in the garden. At first He did not see her as she approached, but, as the moon cast her shadow across the path He looked up and smiled. To Martha it seemed as if the very gates of heaven had opened. Never had she seen such a smile on any face, not even on His. She stood transfixed! Softly He spoke, "Come unto Me...." Instantly Martha was at His feet, sobbing her weary heart out. And even as she wept she knew that He did know everything that was in her heart; she knew that all the doubts and perplexities that clouded her mind were clear to Him.

For some time they remained silent, and as she knelt at His feet, Martha felt that all her grief was dispelled, all her doubts were quieted, and a peace had descended upon her, such as she had never known. Then, as He spoke, she looked up into His face and listened as He explained to her how difficult the path of action was to follow. It was like walking a tightrope—so easy to lose one's balance, because the moment any attachment to the action itself, or to the fruits of the action, entered in, the balance was lost, one fell from the ideal, and by so falling, suffered. And, because attachment brought suffering, Jesus urged Martha to lay her yoke upon Him, and not upon her service to Him, for, as long as one labored for the meat which perished, one would always be dissatisfied, disturbed, and harassed, just as she had been that very day.

How gently, yet how very clearly He had explained what the "good part" was which Mary had chosen. Fundamentally neither sister was superior to the other. Both were right, both were devoted, but each expressed her devotion according to her own temperament and capacity. By her very nature Mary was a contemplative, whereas Martha was active, and found her best expression in service to others. While Mary had united—or yoked—herself to the Christhood of Jesus, in contemplation of Him, Martha had attached herself to Jesus the man through service and devotion to the personality. The "good part" lay in the constant remembrance of God, whether through meditation or through action it did not matter.

As Martha learned all these things, she felt as if her whole life had been completely transformed, so much so, that, from the moment when she left Him, still sitting in the garden, never did she forget Him. She could not. She felt that her mind had become forever united with her Lord's. Everything she did, she did as an offering to Him, until gradually, even as her sister Mary, she too became a contemplative, while yet remaining active. She saw Him in all beings, and served Him in all.

And, now, as she lay resting, it seemed she could hear His voice saying once again: "Well done, thou good and faithful servant...", and she felt as if her whole being had been caught up into that peace which He had promised when He said: "...and you shall find rest unto your soul."

Henry David Thoreau

DOMICILE

My "best" room, however, my withdrawing room, always ready for company, on whose carpet the sun rarely fell, was the pine wood behind my house. Thither in summer days, when distinguished guests came, I took them, and a priceless domestic swept the floor and dusted the furniture and kept the things in order.

Sir James George Frazer

First Fruits

Amongst the Creek Indians of North America, the *busk* or festival of first fruits was the chief ceremony of the year. It was held in July or August, when the corn was ripe, and marked the end of the old year and the beginning of the new one. Before it took place, none of the Indians would eat or even handle any part of the new harvest. Sometimes each town had its own busk; sometimes several towns united to hold one in common. Before celebrating the busk, the people provided themselves with new clothes and new household utensils and furniture; they collected their old clothes and rubbish, together with all the remaining grain and other old provisions, cast them together in one common heap, and consumed them with fire. As a preparation for the ceremony, all the fires in the village were extinguished, and the ashes swept clean away. In particular, the hearth or altar of the temple was dug up and the ashes carried out. Then the chief priest put some roots of the button-snake plant, with some green tobacco leaves and a little of the new fruits, at the bottom of the fireplace, which he afterwards commanded to be covered up with white clay, and wetted over with clean water. A thick arbor of green branches of young trees was then made over the altar. Meanwhile the women at home were cleaning out their houses, renewing the old hearths, and scouring all the cooking vessels that they might be ready to receive the new fire and the new fruits. The public or sacred square was carefully swept of even the smallest crumbs of previous feasts, "for fear of polluting the first fruit offerings." Also every vessel that had contained or had been used about any food during the expiring year was removed from the temple before sunset. Then all the men who were not known to have violated the law of the first fruit offering and that of marriage during the year were summoned by a crier to enter the holy square and observe a solemn fast. But the women (except six old ones), the children, and all who had not attained the rank of warriors were forbidden to enter the square. Sentinels were also posted at the corners of the square to keep out all persons deemed impure and all animals. A strict fast was then observed for two nights and a day, the devotees drinking a bitter decoction of button-snake root "in order to vomit and purge their sinful bodies." That the people outside the square might also be purified, one of the old men laid down a quantity of green tobacco at a corner of the square; this was carried off by an old woman and distributed to the people without, who chewed and swallowed it "in order to afflict their souls." During this general fast, the women, children, and men of weak constitution were allowed to eat after midday, but not before. On the morning when the fast ended, the women brought a quantity of the old year's food to the outside of the sacred square. These provisions were then fetched in and set before the famished multitude, but all traces of them had to be removed before noon. When the sun was declining from the meridian, all the people were commanded by the voice of a crier to stay within doors, to do no bad act, and to be sure to extinguish and throw away every spark of the old fire. Universal silence now reigned. Then the high priest made the new fire by the friction of two pieces of wood, and placed it on the altar under the green arbor. This new fire was believed to atone for all past crimes except murder. Next a basket of new fruits was brought; the high priest took out a little of each sort of fruit, rubbed it with bear's oil, and offered it, together with some flesh, "to the bountiful holy spirit of fire, as a first fruit offering, and an annual oblation for sin." He also consecrated the sacred emetics (the button-snake root and the cassina or black drink) by pouring a little of them into the fire. The persons who had remained outside now approached, without entering, the sacred square; and the chief priest thereupon made a speech, exhorting the people to observe their old rites and customs, announcing that the new divine fire had purged away the sins of the past year, and earnestly warning the women that, if any of them had not extinguished the old fire, or had contracted any impurity, they must forthwith depart, "lest the divine fire should spoil both them and the people." Some of the new fire was then set down outside the holy square; the women carried it home joyfully, and laid it on their unpolluted hearths. When several towns had united to celebrate the festival, the new fire might thus be carried for several miles. The new fruits were then dressed on the new fires and eaten with bear's oil, which was deemed indispensable. At one point of the festival the men rubbed the new corn between their hands, then on their faces and breasts. During the festival which followed, the warriors, dressed in their wild martial array, their heads covered with white down and carrying white feathers in their hands, danced round the sacred arbor, under which burned the new fire. The ceremonies lasted eight days, during which the strictest continence was practiced. Towards the conclusion of the festival the warriors fought a mock battle; then the men and women together, in three circles, danced round the sacred fire. Lastly, all the people smeared themselves with white clay and bathed in running water. They came out of the water believing that no evil could now befall them for what they had done amiss in the past. So they departed in joy and peace.

Otagaki Rengetsu

"REMOVING THE SOOT"

Clearing the soot
From the beams,
Sweeping the dust
From my hearth,
Getting ready for the New Year.

Exodus 12:15 and
Rabbi Lynn Gottlieb

Seven days you shall eat unleavened bread; on the very first day you shall remove leaven from your houses ...

—Exodus 12:15

"Spring Cleaning Ritual on the Eve of the Full Moon Nisan"

Removing the Hametz
In the month of nisan
with the death of winter
and the coming of spring
our ancient mothers
cleaned out their houses.
They gathered brooms, mops, brushes,
rags, stones, and lime
they washed down walls

swept floors
beat rugs
scoured pots
changed over all the dishes in the house.
They opened windows to the sun
hung lines for the airing out of blankets and covers
using fire
air
and water
in the cleaning.
In the month of nisan
before the parting seas
called them out of the old life
our ancient mothers
went down to the river
they went down to the river
to prepare their garments for the spring.
Hands pounded rock
voices drummed out song
there is new life inside us
Shekhinah
prepares for Her birth.
So we labor all women
cleaning and washing
now with our brothers
now with our sons
cleaning the inner house
through the moon of nisan.
On the eve of the full moon
we search our houses
by the light of a candle
for the last trace of winter
for the last crumbs grown stale inside us
for the last darkness still in our hearts.
Washing our hands

we say a blessing
over water …
We light a candle
and search in the listening silence
search the high places
and the low places
inside you
search the attic and the basement
the crevices and crannies
the corners of unused rooms.
Look in your pockets
and the pockets of those around you
for the traces of Mitzrayim.
Some use a feather
some use a knife
to enter the hard places.
Some destroy Hametz with fire
others throw it to the wind
others toss it to the sea.
Look deep for the Hametz
which still gives you pleasure
and cast it to the burning.
When the looking is done
we say:
All that rises up bitter
All that rises up prideful
All that rises up in old ways no longer fruitful
All Hametz still in my possession
but unknown to me
which I have not seen
nor disposed of
may it find common grave
with the dust of the earth
amen amen
selah …

PART NINE

Big Messes

When we look at the actions we perform and the tools we use in everyday housekeeping, we discover within them an inherent ability to improve our world. We can sweep away poverty by reaching out and sharing things both tangible and intangible with other people. We can wash away the stains and blood of war and crime by cleansing our hearts of prejudice and developing compassion for those unlike ourselves; and we can pray to whatever it is that we hold sacred, carefully and deliberately ordering our words so that they will manifest goodness in the universe.

Perhaps all of the various tasks associated with housecleaning are practice. Practice so that when we're confronted with the truly big messes—war, natural disaster, the effects of irresponsibility on our world—we've internalized rituals we can use to effectively take care of the matters at hand. Examining our sense of conscientiousness toward our homes leads us to consider the possibilities we might discover if we were to impose those feelings onto our world, as author Mary Catherine Bateson suggests. If we start thinking of Earth as our home, too, then we will work a little harder toward bettering it.

Acknowledging the events that go on in the world—the crises, the disasters, the unforeseeable tragedies—that are outside of our control helps us focus on what we can change, while we learn to accept those things that we cannot. Evangelist Hannah Whitall Smith explains that, "this world is God's housekeeping." The answers to our questions of *why* may lie in understanding that God's plans for our lives and our world are bigger than our own—and we, as humans, are incapable of understanding God's ways.

If one way of coping with the big messes is to relinquish control to God, another approach is to imagine all we would do to clean up our planet if we could. Poet Allen Ginsberg, through his extended metaphor of housekeeping, urges us to take responsibility for what has happened, from war to pollution, and to take action, working toward a remedy for all the troubles humanity has imposed on itself.

When our personal environments are ravaged by fear and terror, many of us act on an internalized impulse—an urge to clean up the mess. Cleaning becomes both a means of grieving and a path toward hope as we scrub our way toward understanding a situation that we can never change. For author Andrea Barrett, wiping up the ash from her windowsill after the events of September 11, 2001, becomes profound when she realizes she touches more than dust, but also "the ash of people," the cumulative suffering resulting from the tragedy.

Exposure to any kind of trauma irrevocably changes people—who they were before witnessing or experiencing fear of that caliber is not who they are afterward. Starhawk's account of restoring order to a Palestinian home after it is violently searched by Israeli soldiers illustrates her intrinsic need to clean up in an attempt to re-create a sense of safety within the physical environment, and within herself, that, while present before the search, will never be the same again.

War and its affects on those who witness it sully even the lives of those who don't experience combat firsthand. A sense of normalcy is all but destroyed, as depicted by veteran and author John Crawford—who yearned to be home cleaning up after his puppy, rather than taking care of the bloody messes that war made seem so routine. Normalcy is replaced with something else, something intangible, something we can never be rid of until war becomes a thing of the past, a faint, dark memory.

In seeing in the act of cleaning an attempt to re-create not only a physical home, but also a sense of security, safety, and love that a home evokes, we discover the nurturing aspects naturally a part of so many of the daily chores we perform. As American poet Eric Leigh paints a picture of the repercussions of war, he describes a mother and son who mine the "space / between night and day, ritual and work" tending to the grandfather—a broken man haunted by the cruelty he witnessed while at war—in much the same way a child is cared for. Through their gift of cleanliness and order, the mother and son cannot restore what the grandfather has lost, but they can fortify his living space with their strength, loyalty, and love—a gift of their hearts.

The voices in this section sensitize us to the resounding global impact our everyday actions can have. As we realize the holy in the mundane, we are empowered to respond to the tragedies of our communities, our country, and our world, knowing that even our smallest gestures—one windowsill dusted, one path swept, one dish washed—can contribute to saving it, one sacred action at a time.

Mary Catherine Bateson

Ecopoiesis

What we need today is not to apply more technology to housework, or even to teach those who do housework to avoid non-biodegradable detergents or aerosols. We must transform our attitude toward all productive work and toward the planet into expressions of homemaking, where we create and sustain the possibility of life. It may take yet another new word to express the single responsibility that unites the homemaker, male or female, with the men and women who mine and plant and create industries and work for effective forms of exchange and for a peaceful world. Such a new term might be *ecopoiesis*, using the Greek root for *making* that gives us the word *poetry*. Still, the making of words or rhymes is insufficient; the problem is with our understanding of the materialities that make life possible: the forests and the cooking pots, the necessary recuperation time of fields and workers, the private spaces of our lives where the spirit flourishes, and the woodlands that are still wild.

Hannah Whitall Smith

"Comfort"

A great many things in God's divine providences do not look like goodness to the eye of sense, and in reading the Psalms we wonder perhaps how the psalmist could say, after some of the things he records, "for his mercy endureth forever." But faith sits down before mysteries such as these, and says, "The Lord is good, therefore all that He does must be good, no matter how it looks, and I can wait for His explanations."

A housekeeping illustration has often helped me here. If I have a friend whom I know to be a good housekeeper, I do not trouble over the fact that at housecleaning time things in her house may seem to be more or less upset, carpets up, and furniture shrouded in coverings, and even perhaps painting and decorating making some rooms uninhabitable. I say to myself, "My friend is a good housekeeper, and although things look so uncomfortable now, all this upset is only because she means in the end to make it far more comfortable than ever it was before." This world is God's housekeeping; and although things at present look grievously upset, yet, since we know that He is good, and therefore must be a good Housekeeper, we may be perfectly sure that all this present upset is only to bring about in the end a far better state of things than could have been without it. I dare say we have all felt at times as though we could have done God's housekeeping better than He does it Himself, but, when we realize that God is good, we can feel this no longer. And it comforts me enormously, when the world seems to me to be going all wrong, just to say to myself, "It is not my housekeeping, but it is the Lord's; and the Lord is good, therefore His housekeeping must be good too; and it is foolish for me to trouble."

Allen Ginsberg

"HOMEWORK"

Homage to Kenneth Koch

> *If I were doing my Laundry I'd wash my dirty Iran*
> *I'd throw in my United States, and pour on the Ivory Soap,*
> *scrub up Africa, put all the birds and elephants back in*
> *the jungle,*
> *I'd wash the Amazon river and clean the oily Carib & Gulf of*
> *Mexico,*
> *Rub that smog off the North Pole, wipe up all the pipelines*
> *in Alaska,*
> *Rub a dub dub for Rocky Flats and Los Alamos, Flush that*
> *sparkly Cesium out of Love Canal*
> *Rinse down the Acid Rain over the Parthenon & Sphinx,*
> *Drain the Sludge out of the Mediterranean basin &*
> *make it azure again,*
> *Put some blueing back into the sky over the Rhine, bleach*
> *the little Clouds so snow return white as snow,*
> *Cleanse the Hudson Thames & Neckar, Drain the Suds out*
> *of Lake Erie*

*Then I'd throw big Asia in one giant Load & wash out the
    blood & Agent Orange,*
Dump the whole mess of Russia and China in the wringer,
*squeeze out the tattletale Gray of U.S. Central American
    police state,*
*& put the planet in the drier & let it sit 20 minutes or an Aeon
    till it came out clean.*

Andrea Barrett

ASH

Tuesday

What kind of a city was this where a plane—no, two planes—could crash into a building? I think I thought that; truly, everything that happened that day is muddled. I saw the second one hit while I was walking home from the dog-sitter's. The pilot had fallen asleep, the air-traffic system was down, someone had made an awful and clumsy mistake, and something I couldn't imagine had happened. A hijacking never crossed my mind. I was too naive to think that thought. But in a city where it sometimes seemed that nothing worked—in Brooklyn, I had told my family, everything is broken—a mistake of even this magnitude seemed possible.

It was my upstairs neighbor, leaning out the window and shouting down to me—I must have run to our building—who first used the word "they": some "they" had attacked the second tower. But who were "they"? Nothing he said made sense. My husband, now framed in our front window, looked similarly puzzled; I ran upstairs and we turned on the TV. Somewhere during those minutes, we also first heard the words "terrorist" and "hijacking." We looked out the window again. Then at the TV. Then we ran up to the roof.

In our part of Williamsburg, the East River is only a block and a half away and the buildings are low, a mixture of warehouses, three and four story tenements, and industrial buildings. Nothing impedes the view of the jagged wall of stone and metal across the river, so near it seems one can touch it. The other tenants—two young Brits, a photographer and a filmmaker; a ballet dancer from Mexico and her musician boyfriend; the older French photographer who'd called down to me—were already up on the roof, staring at what had always dominated the sky. Smoke rose from the towers; flames began to shoot from the sides; by then we were crying. The builder and a friend appeared, also some neighbors from next door, while the Brits, who had cell phones, called their families in London to say they were alive. All over the world, I realized, this must be on TV; in Florida, my mother would be terrified. I ran downstairs to call her.

When I returned, what I saw was impossible. Someone tried to explain it to me—the south tower had collapsed while I was gone—but I couldn't hear it; I turned again and again to the sight and each time covered my eyes and turned away. Where had the tower gone? Soon the builder said, in a low, sad voice, "Shit. There goes the other one," and when I opened my eyes I saw the second tower unmaking itself, the sides curling away from the middle like skin peeling off a banana, the smoke spewing upward until everything was gone.

Why talk about the rest of that morning, the rest of that day? All of us were glued alternately to the desecrated skyline and the television, watching the same images again and again, each minute more deeply aware of the people who'd been inside those towers and what had happened to them. The trains closed down, the city closed down. No one knew what to do or say. At two that afternoon, the L train opened; Barry took his camera and went into Manhattan, working his way farther and farther downtown—so far that he was uncomfortably close to Building #7 when it came down. When he returned that evening to fetch more film, he convinced me to go back in with him. I should see this, he said. The way so much of daily life was still being lived; the tremendous social momentum that keeps us moving through the forms of life even after the heart has stopped. I would, he said, find the people and the sight of what still stood consoling. While I didn't believe that, I knew that if I didn't go into Manhattan soon I would never go there again. I'd put the dog and cat in the car and start driving and never stop—as if I could drive away from this, or that it would matter, now, where I lived.

Below Houston, then below Canal: closed streets, tired cops, an endless line of trucks and bulldozers and cranes and flatbed trailers mounded with lights and generators, machines whose names I don't know parked end to end with their engines running and their headlights on, a procession that stretched for miles and seemed to pulse with longing to get going, to do something, to move toward their grim tasks; prevented from that by the fires burning at what was already being termed Ground Zero. But also, among the tired firemen trudging toward the nearest open subway station at West Fourth Street, between the young police cadets and the Port Authority workers and the volunteer nurses and EMTs, we saw people walking dogs, pushing babies in strollers, sitting in bars and talking earnestly over supper and drinks. People on bikes. People holding hands. People unable not to do what they had always done, in the neighborhoods where they made their homes; people moving about, people living.

Where North Moore intersects with West Street, volunteers had gathered; meaning to see what we could do, we joined the crowd. Cots and stretchers filled a courtyard rimmed with face masks, bottled water, food, all sorts of supplies. No one walked or crawled or was carried from the rubble and there was nothing for the rest of us to do. We could see the fire burning, still. The smoke was lashing through the crowd, the trucks still waited helplessly. So did we.

Wednesday, Thursday, Friday

We watch the TV, we read the papers, we watch the TV, we read the papers. We talk to people on the streets and in bars and cafes. At dusk we stand on abandoned lots at the river shore along with everyone else. We used to walk the dog here at night, in the silent but pleasant company of others who, like us, had picked their way through the broken grass and the holes in the fence, around the garbage and over the rocks, to get a taste of the breeze blowing up the river and the sight of the city, so close. Now there are hundreds of people here, faces glimpsed before at windows or the subway platform or the park. In silent ranks, we watch the sun set over the smoking hole. The first night the cloud of smoke blew east, over Brooklyn Heights, and we could hardly smell it. But the wind has shifted since then and, as the sun sets, the smoke drapes Manhattan like a scarf and slides across the water into our nostrils.

It rains on Thursday night, after bolts of lightning first strike so close by that sparks fly and our next-door neighbor's television and amplifier are fried: a steady, unrelenting rain pushed toward us by a strong wind blowing up the river. Before I think to close the front windows (which face the bridge, and used to face the towers), the rain pours through the screens, all over the sill, and down the wall to the floor. I wipe up what I can. The next morning, I head for the sill with a rag, having learned during my first city rainstorm that each drop coming through the screens leaves behind a dot of the filth it has carried from the air. Now the entire sill is dark gray, six linear feet of grime. What I dab comes up like ash and as I back away, the rag still in my hand, I realize that's what it is: ash of buildings, ash of planes. The ash of people ...

Marsha Norman

WOMEN'S WORK

As women, our historical role has been to clean up the mess. Whether it's the mess left by war or death or children or sickness. I think the violence you see in plays by women is a direct reflection of that historical role. We are not afraid to look under the bed, or to wash the sheets; we know that life is messy. We know that somebody has to clean it up, and that only if it is cleaned up can we hope to start over, and get better.

Starhawk

RESTORING ORDER

The soldiers order us all into one room and then close the door. We can hear banging and loud thuds against the walls as they search the house. I am trying to think of something to sing to distract us, to keep the spirits of the children up, but my voice won't work. Neta teaches us a silly children's song in Arabic: "The train comes, the train goes," she sings, "The train is full of sugar and tea." The delighted children begin to sing. Hanin and I drum on the tables as the soldiers are throwing things around in the other room. Little Ahmed begins to dance. When we put him up on the table he smiles and swings his hips and makes us all laugh.

When the soldiers finally leave, we emerge to examine the damage. Everything has been pulled off the walls and thrown out of the closets into huge piles. The paneling is full of holes. The floor is covered with broken glass, and bags of grain have been emptied in the sink.

We begin to clean up.

We are a houseful of women and know how to restore order. Melissa sweeps while Jessica keeps the children out of the glass. I help Hanin clear a path in the bedroom, folding the clothes of her absent husband, hanging up her own things, finding the secret sexy underwear the soldiers have obviously examined. When the house is back together, Hanin and Samar start to cook. The grandmother is having a high blood pressure attack, and we lay her down on the couch. I sit down, utterly exhausted, as Hanin and the women serve a meal. A few porcelain birds and artificial flowers are back in their places. Somehow once again the house feels like a sanctuary.

John Crawford

"No Crying in Baseball"

The satellite phone was hot against my cheek. It was barely ten A.M. and already the temperature was soaring into the triple digits. "C'mon, answer. Answer." On the fourth mechanical ring, I heard a barely audible "Hello."

"Hey, darling," I said in my sweetest voice, scarcely able to contain my excitement. I had been away from home for eight months [in Iraq], and no matter how many times I called, I always got shivers any time my wife answered the phone.

"Oh, hey." I could hear the tension in her voice. I prepared myself for the worst.

"Is everything okay?" I realized I was holding my breath in anticipation. When all you have time to do is worry about what is going on at home, you start to imagine some terrible things.

"No." She let out a long dramatic sigh and then continued. "Murphy shit all over the house, ate the cushions on the sofa and a pair of my shoes, and I've only been gone for a couple hours."

I tried unsuccessfully to suppress a smile, sure she could hear it. She had bought that puppy before we were married, and over a year later it was still a monster.

"I'm sorry, hon." I gave her my best sympathetic voice, but I think its insensitivity was detected.

"Fuck, more piss!" Stephanie blurted out and I imagined she stumbled onto another sticky puddle.

"Well, it could be worse. I mean, I'd give anything to be at home cleaning up dog shit."

"What could be grosser than cleaning up a house full of dog shit?" The disgust in her voice was palpable.

"Try cleaning up brains." I tried to catch the words and pull them back even as they left my mouth. It's hard living with a bunch of soldiers and then trying to talk like a normal person to your wife on the phone.

"When did you clean up brains? Tell me about it, I want to know." There was curiosity and naiveté in her voice, but the self-pity was gone. *What can it hurt?* So I told her about my day.

Eric Leigh

"LAST OF THE MIDNIGHT LULLABIES"

Middle of the night, my grandfather calls
stuck again in that foxhole,
his buddy's head shot straight off.

Or he thinks he's still in the asylum
where the only sounds he heard were those
from the past—stray bullets, his own sobs.

Now, when he cries my mother's name,
he does so as if she was a child in danger
and he—the father he never was.

In five minutes, we're on our way
down the same back roads we drove years before,
taking my dad to his second-shift,

those graveyard hours I sat in the back,
my mother telling me to sleep. But there is no
going back to the peace of what was.

When we arrive, my mother kills the headlights
and begins doing what she does best.
There's no wrinkled sheet her hands can't smooth,

no ruined blouse or man she can't rescue
with club soda or her touch.
The truth lives just beneath her perfume:

hold a man long enough and eventually he'll cry;
hold him longer and he'll stop. We find him
on the couch in his tattered robe

and old man slippers, empty bottle at his side.
"Warm him some milk," my mother says,
and I do what I'm told as she goes to him

and strokes his head, hums him that lullaby,
the one she made up out of his absence
and the nights her mother worked,

out of a need to calm herself and a farmhouse
full of children. Some part of her is still that girl
in worn-through shoes, wandering

from room to room, checking the eyes
of every child to make sure that they're sleeping.
Memory lane is a minefield of twice-learned lessons.

Consider this: it was an early frost just like this one
when he plucked a fallen wasp-nest from the ground
to help me kill my fear.

How he peeled back the paper of a cell
and coaxed a worker from its bed.
Impossible still—the way the wasp crawled

up his thumb and threw itself to the wind,
how those moments we're woken from
stay with us and stay true.

When he's still, we cover him with blankets.
Maybe now he'll forget enough to fall asleep,
as we stand at the kitchen sink, mining the space

between night and day, ritual and work.
I wash. She dries. We both look straight ahead,
cleaning up another mess and staring down the dawn.

Ashley Isaacson

"OFFERING"

I found the crucifix buried in the dirt under a pile of heavy bricks. We had been digging through the heap of rubble that was all that remained of Miss Margaret Brou's house. The crucifix was about eight inches tall, with a Jesus figure whose arms had broken off, but whose feet were still nailed to the cross. I could tell it was not just a toy, as it was made of some kind of metal, bronze maybe. I reverently brushed the dirt aside. I took it to the elderly and disabled Miss Margaret, who had been watching our work. "Miss Margaret, I found this," I said. With tears in her eyes, she thanked me and took the crucifix, setting it tenderly on the cushion of her walker. I asked if it was special to her. "Yes," she replied. "It came from my mother's casket." I put my arm around her. "God bless you," she said. "And you," I replied softly. It had come from her mother's casket, and I had pulled it from the dirt under a pile of bricks.

Miss Margaret's house was on the border of the first marsh that we restored. There were two kinds of debris cluttering the marsh: There were fallen tree limbs and driftwood, and then there were the objects of human origin: water heaters, bathtubs, plastic bags, photo albums, linoleum, t-shirts and telephones. We removed the second kind from the marsh, but left the first, because it was part of nature's grand plan. It would prevent flooding and erosion, and eventually decay and feed back into the ecosystem. Nature knew what it was doing with a hurricane.

A few weeks ago, Professor Matthew Myer Boulton asked our class to discuss whether one could confess on behalf of others. I questioned the redemptive power in that, supposing that other than nurturing a sense of compassion and solidarity with the sinner, there would be little point. But as I untangled countless plastic bags from tree branches, as I dug shingles and paint cans and vinyl records out of the muddy marsh, something changed. It may not have been my trash, but I felt spontaneously arising in myself this prayer: "I am sorry. I am sorry that we do this."

At the end of the day there was a beautiful green marsh where before there had been, in essence, a junkyard. I knew that the few bags of trash I hauled out of the marsh could be seen as insignificant. And yet, my efforts felt like an offering.

Stephen Vincent Benét

"PRAYER"

Grant us a common faith that man shall know bread and peace—that he shall know justice and righteousness, freedom and security, an equal opportunity and an equal chance to do his best not only in our own lands, but throughout the world. And in that faith let us march toward the clean world our hands can make.

ACKNOWLEDGMENTS

So many people encouraged, supported, and championed me as I composed *Next to Godliness*. What gifts!

Huge gratitude to Wendy Schmalz, extraordinary friend and agent, who was unfaltering in her faith in my book and in me, and found the perfect home for both.

Vast thanks as well to all of the kind people at SkyLight Paths Publishing—Maura Shaw, Melanie Robinson, Emily Wichland, and, especially, Jessica Swift, who is the true heroine of *Next to Godliness*.

Arthur Goldwag took me seriously even when I didn't, and he guided me to some of the finest pieces in this book.

Marc Poirier was one of the first people to "get it" and proved the depth of his understanding by contributing his beautiful essay.

Fred Courtright led me through the labyrinth of permissions.

Deep appreciation to all of the writers I work with in my book-doctoring incarnation. Each provides inspiration in so many ways every day. (You're all my favorites!)

Thanks as well to Myotai Sensei, Molly, Lauren, Julia, Judy, Hattie, Hannah, Grace, and my family, for insights and help along the way.

And in loving memory of Louis Keller, whose books on Buddhism and spirituality were some of the very first I read, and who always did the dishes.

CREDITS

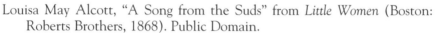

Orion Press, Inc. First published as a Beacon paperback in 1969 by arrangement with Grossman Publishers, Inc.

"Maud Martha Spares the Mouse" from *Maud Martha*, by Gwendolyn Brooks. Copyright © 1993 by Gwendolyn Brooks. Published by Third World Press of Chicago. Reprinted by consent of Brooks Permissions.

"Doing the Dishes" from *Around the House and in the Garden: A Memoir of Heartbreak, Healing, and Home Improvement* by Dominique Browning. Reprinted with the permission of Scribner, an imprint of Simon & Schuster Adult Publishing Group. Copyright © 2002 by Dominique Browning. All rights reserved.

"Kavvanah for Cleaning" from *The Jewish Spirit Journal* 1, No. 2 (February 1999). Copyright © 1999 by Yitzhak Buxbaum. All rights reserved. Reprinted with the permission of Yitzhak Buxbaum.

Lydia Maria Child, excerpt from *The American Frugal Housewife* (1829). Public Domain.

Joan Chittister, excerpt from *The Rule of Benedict: Insight for the Ages*, The Crossroad Publishing Company, 1997. Copyright © 1992 by Joan D. Chittister, OSB.

Billy Collins, "Advice to Writers" from *Sailing Around the Room* (New York: Random House, 2001). Originally collected in *The Apple that Astonished Paris* (Fayetteville: University of Arkansas Press, 1996).

Amiya Corbin, "Martha" [1,305 words] from *Vedanta for the Western World* (Hollywood: Vedanta Press, 1945).

Excerpt from *The Last True Story I'll Ever Tell* by John Crawford, copyright © 2005 by John Crawford. Used by permission of Riverhead Books, an imprint of Penguin Group (USA), Inc.

Selection from *On Pilgrimage* by Dorothy Day courtesy of Dorothy Day Library on the Web at http://www.catholicworker.org/dorothyday/.

Shoghi Effendi, excerpt [165 words] from Chapter VIII: "Bahá'u'lláh's Banishment to Iraq" from *God Passes By*. (US Bahá'í Publishing Trust). Reprinted with the permission of the Bahá'í World Centre.

Sir James George Frazer (1854–1941), excerpt from *The Golden Bough*. New York: The Macmillan Company, 1900. Project Gutenberg Copyright Status: Not copyrighted in the United States.

Mohandas K. Gandhi, excerpt from *The Collected Works of Mahatma Gandhi* (New Delhi: Publications Division, Ministry of Information and Broadcasting, 1958). Reprinted 1969, 2000.

"I Stop Writing the Poem" from *Moon Crossing Bridge*. Copyright © 1992 by Tess Gallagher. Reprinted with the permission of Graywolf Press, Saint Paul, Minnesota.

Allen Ginsberg, "Homework" from *Selected Poems*. Copyright © 1981 by Allen Ginsberg. Reprinted with the permission of HarperCollins Publishers and Penguin Group (UK) Ltd.

Credits

———."A Plain Talk as to Securing Negro Homes," a statement in the *Washington Colored American* [Washington, D.C. August 24, 1901]. University of Illinois Press: The Booker T. Washington Papers Volume 6: 1901–1902. Open Book Edition © 1977 University of Illinois Press. http://www. historycooperative.org/btw/Vol.6/html/188.html.

Jessamyn West, excerpt from *Hide and Seek* (New York: Harcourt Brace Jovanovich, 1973). Copyright © 1973 by Jessamyn West, renewed in 2001 by Ann Cash.

"Love Calls Us to the Things of This World" from *Things of This World*, copyright © 1956 and renewed 1984 by Richard Wilbur, reprinted by permission of Harcourt, Inc.

Virginia Woolf (1882–1941) excerpt from *Night and Day*, first published in England by Duckworth & Co., 1919. First published in the United States by Doran, 1920. Project Gutenberg Copyright Status: Not copyrighted in the United States.

Anzia Yezierska (1885–1970) excerpt from *Hungry Hearts* (Penguin Twentieth-Century Classics). First Published in the United States by the Houghton Mifflin Company, 1920.

These pages constitute a continuation of the copyright page. Every effort has been made to trace and acknowledge copyright holders of all the material included in this anthology. The editor apologizes for any errors or omissions that may remain and asks that any omissions be brought to her attention so that they may be corrected in future editions. Please send corrections to:

Alice Peck
c/o SkyLight Paths Publishing
Sunset Farms Offices
Route 4, P.O. Box 237
Woodstock, VT 05091

ABOUT THE
CONTRIBUTORS

Louisa May Alcott (1832–88) was determined to contribute to her family's income and worked as a servant, a seamstress, and a Civil War nurse before she made her fortune as a writer. She is the author of many books, including the children's classic, *Little Women*.

Gaston Bachelard (1884–1962) was one of France's leading philosophers. He is the author of the classic *The Poetics of Space* as well as *The Psychoanalysis of Fire* and *The Poetics of Reverie*.

James Baldwin's (1924–1987) first novel, *Go Tell It on the Mountain*, was rooted in his experiences as a young preacher. Born in Harlem, he lived much of his life in Paris. His novel *Another Country* received critical acclaim, as did his essays in *The Fire Next Time*.

Andrea Barrett received the National Book Award for her novel, *Ship Fever*, in 1996. In 2001 she was given a MacArthur fellowship. Barrett teaches at the MFA program for writers at Warren Wilson College in Asheville, North Carolina.

Mary Catherine Bateson has written several books on linguistic and anthropological topics, including *Composing a Life* and *With a Daughter's Eye: A Memoir of Margaret Mead and Gregory Bateson*.

Jeannette Batz has been a staff writer on the *RiverFront Times* for many years and is the author of *Half Life: What We Gave Up to Work* and *The Broom Closet*.

Sue Bender is the author of *Plain and Simple: A Woman's Journey to the Amish*. In *Everyday Sacred: A Woman's Journey Home*, Bender, a former therapist, chronicles her struggle to bring her experiences with the Amish to her hectic days at home.

Stephen Vincent Benét (1898–1943) was an American poet and author who is most famous for *John Brown's Body*, a long narrative poem of the Civil War that won the Pulitzer Prize, and his story, "The Devil and Daniel Webster."

Henri Bosco (1888–1976) was a French writer and the author of *Le Jardin d'Hyacinthe* and *Le Mas Théotime*, which received the Prix Renaudot in 1945.

Sarah Ban Breathnach is the author of *Simple Abundance: A Daybook of Comfort and Joy* as well as several other books in the *Simple Abundance* series. She is also the founder of the Simple Abundance Charitable Trust.

Gwendolyn Brooks (1917–2000) was the first African American to be awarded the Pulitzer Prize for poetry in 1950 for her book *Annie Allen*. Brooks was named Poet Laureate of the state of Illinois in 1968 and appointed to the prestigious National Institute of Arts and Letters in 1976.

Dominique Browning has been the editor of *House & Garden* magazine since 1995. She lives in New York.

Yitzhak Buxbaum is the author of numerous publications and has taught at CAJE conferences, Havurah Movement Summer Institutes, the Elat Chayyim Jewish Retreat Center, the New York Open Center, and the New School for Social Research.

Lydia Maria Child (1802–1880) was a novelist, reporter, and ardent advocate of women's rights. She was the author of *The American Frugal Housewife*.

Joan Chittister, OSB, is the executive director of Benetvision: A Research and Resource Center for Contemporary Spirituality, located in Erie, Pennsylvania. She is the author of more than twenty books, including *The Rule of Benedict* and *The Story of Ruth*.

Billy Collins is the author of six collections of poetry, including *Sailing Alone Around the Room*. He is a distinguished professor of English at Lehman College of the City University of New York. He was Poet Laureate of the United States from 2001–2003.

Amiya Corbin (1902–1986), later the Countess of Sandwich, was a student of Swami Prabhavananda and devoted the first part of her life to the development of the Vedanta Society of Southern California. Her writings were published in *Vedanta for the Western World*.

John Crawford was newly married and working toward a B.A. in anthropology when his National Guard unit was sent to Iraq. He now lives in Florida, where he is completing his degree and writing.

The Dalai Lama, His Holiness the 14th Dalai Lama, Tenzin Gyatso, is the head of state and the spiritual leader of the Tibetan people. He was awarded the Nobel Prize for peace in 1989.

Dorothy Day (1897–1980) was an American journalist turned social activist, anarchist, and devout member of the Catholic Church. Alongside Peter Maurin, she founded the Catholic Worker Movement in 1933, espousing nonviolence and hospitality for the impoverished and downtrodden.

Shoghi Effendi (1897–1957) was guardian of the Bahá'í faith and interpreter of its teachings. He translated many of the writings of Bahá'u'lláh and 'Abdu'l-Bahá into English, expounded their meanings, and encouraged the establishment of Bahá'í institutions throughout the world.

Rick Fields (1942–1999) was a respected journalist and leading authority on American Buddhism. He published several books, including *How the Swans Came to the Lake: A Narrative History of Buddhism in America* and *Instructions to the Cook.*

Sir James George Frazer (1854–1941) was a Scottish classicist and anthropologist, and is known especially for his masterpiece, *The Golden Bough*, a monumental study in comparative folklore, magic, and religion.

Tess Gallagher is a poet, essayist, novelist, and playwright. Her honors include a fellowship from the Guggenheim Foundation, two National Endowment of the Arts awards, and the Elliston Award for "best book of poetry published by a small press" for the collection *Instructions to the Double.*

Mahatma Gandhi (1869–1948) was instrumental in India's drive for independence from Britain and recognized for his use of methods of passive resistance and nonviolent disobedience to influence British rulers.

Allen Ginsberg (1926–1997) was an American poet and outspoken member of the Beat generation. His volumes of poetry include *Kaddish and Other Poems: 1958–60, Collected Poems: 1947–1980,* and *White Shroud: Poems 1980–85.*

Bernard Glassman is abbot of the Zen Community of New York and also the Zen Center of Los Angeles. He is a former aerospace engineer and the cofounder of the Zen Peacemaker Order.

Johann Wolfgang von Goethe (1749–1832) was a German writer, scientist, and philosopher. As a writer, Goethe was one of the paramount figures of German literature and European Romanticism. He was the author of *Faust* and *Theory of Colors.*

Rabbi Lynn Gottlieb was the first woman ordained in the Jewish Renewal Movement. In 1983, she moved to Albuquerque, New Mexico, where she cofounded Congregation Nahalat Shalom. Gottlieb currently lives in Southern California, where she heads Interfaith Inventions.

Thich Nhat Hanh, a Buddhist monk since the age of sixteen, has been living in exile from his Vietnamese homeland for more than thirty years. He is a noted advocate of peace and has written more than seventy-five books of prose, poetry, and prayers.

Nathaniel Hawthorne (1804–1864) is best known for *The Scarlet Letter, The House of the Seven Gables*, and *The Blithedale Romance*.

Brother Lawrence (Nicholas Herman c.1605–1691) was born in Lorraine province, France. After serving as a soldier and a footman, he entered the religious community of the Carmelites. While in the community, he worked in the kitchen. His writings were edited after his death by Abbé de Beaufort and printed in two volumes: *Maximes Spirituelles* and *Moeurs et Entretiens du Frère Laurent*.

Homer (c.700 B.C.E.) is a principal figure of ancient Greek literature and considered the first European poet. Two epic poems are attributed to Homer—the *Iliad* and the *Odyssey*.

Ashley Isaacson was one of a group of Harvard Divinity School students that traveled to Ocean Springs, Mississippi, in the spring of 2006 as part of the ongoing effort to rebuild a Gulf Coast region ravaged by Hurricane Katrina.

The Reverend Dr. Martin Luther King, Jr. (1929–1968) was a Nobel Laureate, a Baptist minister, and an African American civil rights activist. He is revered as one of the greatest leaders and heroes in America's history and in the history of nonviolence.

Dorianne Laux is the author of three collections of poetry: *Smoke, What We Carry*, and *Awake*. She received a fellowship from the National Endowment for the Arts and is an associate professor at the University of Oregon's Program in Creative Writing.

Ursula K. Le Guin has published six books of poetry, twenty novels, more than one hundred short stories, four collections of essays, eleven books for children, and four volumes of translation. Her best-known fantasy works, the first four *Books of Earthsea*, have sold millions of copies.

Eric Leigh received his MFA in poetry from the University of Michigan where he was honored with Hopwood Awards in poetry and nonfiction as well as a Cowden Fellowship. His recent awards include the "Discovery"/The Nation Prize, the New Letters Prize for Poetry, and the Robinson Jeffers Tor House Prize for Poetry. His work has appeared or is forthcoming in *The Nation, Third Coast, New Letters, Cimarron Review, Salt Hill*, and *Passages North*. He currently resides in San Francisco, California.

Jarvis Jay Masters is a widely published African American Buddhist writer living on San Quentin's death row. A growing international movement is seeking to overturn his conviction for his participation in the killing of a prison guard; many believe Masters was incorrectly and unfairly convicted.

Cheryl Mendelson has practiced law in New York City and taught philosophy at Purdue and Columbia universities. She is the author of *Home Comforts: The Art and Science of Homemaking* and a novel, *Morningside Heights*.

Mother Teresa (1910–1997) was an Albanian-born Roman Catholic missionary in India and the author of *Carriers of Christ's Love* and *A Gift for God.* She received the Nobel Prize for peace in 1979 for her humanitarian work among lepers and the poor of Calcutta.

Pablo Neruda (1904–1973) was a Chilean diplomat as well as one of the most influential poets of the twentieth century. Some of his most beloved poems are the *Odes to Common Things,* collected in several volumes. In 1971, Neruda was awarded the Nobel Prize for literature.

Marsha Norman's play *'night, Mother* won the Pulitzer Prize and four Tony Award nominations. Four years later, she published her first novel, *The Fortune Teller,* and followed it with *Four Plays* and *The Secret Garden,* a Broadway musical.

Gunilla Norris lives in Mystic, Connecticut, where she works as a writer, meditation teacher, and psychotherapist in private practice. She is the author of *Becoming Bread* and *Being Home.*

Kathleen Norris is the author of the award-winning bestsellers *The Cloister Walk* and *Dakota: A Spiritual Geography.* Her personal narratives, essays, and poetry have been published in a wide range of anthologies, magazines, and journals.

Kakuzo Okakura (1863–1919) was a scholar, respected art critic, and curator of the Chinese and Japanese art collection at the Boston Museum of Fine Arts. He devoted his life to the preservation and reawakening of traditional Japanese culture.

Marc Poirier is a professor of law at Seton Hall Law School. He served as president of the Committee on Hydroelectric Regulation of the Federal Energy Bar Association and has published in the areas of energy, environmental and constitutional law, and coastal land use.

Louise Rafkin is the author of *Other People's Dirt: A Housecleaner's Curious Adventures,* for which she received a National Endowment for the Arts award. Her articles regularly appear on Salon.com and in the *New York Times Magazine.* She writes and records commentary for *All Things Considered.*

Otagaki Rengetsu (1791–1875) was renowned as a *waka* poet, producing hundreds of verses, and also as a painter and potter. Rengetsu was raised as a samurai lady, lost two husbands and all her children to illness, and became a Buddhist nun at age thirty-three.

Rainer Maria Rilke (1875–1926) is one of the most important poets of the twentieth century and author of *The Duino Elegies, Letters to a Young Poet,* and *Sonnets to Orpheus,* as well as his prose piece, *The Notebook of Malte Laurids Brigge.*

Marilynne Robinson is the author of *Housekeeping,* regarded by many as an American classic; it received the PEN/Hemingway Award for best first novel and was nominated for the Pulitzer Prize. *Gilead*, her second novel, was published in 2004.

Taigu Ryokan (1759–1831) is one of the most popular figures in Japanese Buddhist history. As a poet-monk, Ryokan followed a life of mendicancy in the countryside and expressed himself through poems.

Hannah Whitall Smith (1832–1911) was an American evangelist and reformer, a major public speaker, and a writer in the Holiness Movement of the late nineteenth century.

Starhawk is the author of nine books, including her best-selling *The Spiral Dance*, *The Pagan Book of Living and Dying*, and *Webs of Power*, winner of the 2003 Nautilus Award for social change. She is a regular contributor to BeliefNet.com and Znet (zmag.org).

Henry David Thoreau (1817–1862) was an author and naturalist, and one of the most influential figures in American thought and literature. His books *Walden* and *Civil Disobedience* are considered classics.

Gary Thorp is the author of *Sweeping Changes: Discovering the Joy of Zen in Everyday Tasks*. He was lay-ordained in the lineage of Shunryu Suzuki Roshi. A former bookseller and jazz pianist, Thorp is a full-time writer, doing research in marine biology and the ecology of mountain lions.

Chogyam Trungpa Rinpoche (1939–1987) was a Tibetan Buddhist meditation master and the founder and president of Vajradhatu, Naropa Institute, and Shambhala Training. His books include *The Myth of Freedom* and *Shambhala: The Sacred Path of the Warrior*.

Booker T. Washington (1856–1915) was an African American educator who headed Tuskegee Institute. The best known of his many books is *Up from Slavery*. Washington was counted among the ablest public speakers of his time.

Jessamyn West (1902–1984) was a noted Quaker author who wrote for numerous periodicals, including *The New Yorker*. She was the author of several books, including *The Friendly Persuasion; Hide & Seek;* and *Cress Delahanty*.

Richard Wilbur's books of poetry include *New and Collected Poems*, which won the Pulitzer Prize, and *Things of This World*, for which he received the Pulitzer Prize and the National Book Award. He was U.S. Poet Laureate, elected a chevalier of the *Ordre des Palmes Académiques*, and is a chancellor emeritus of The Academy of American Poets.

Virginia Woolf (1882–1941) was a British author, a feminist, a significant figure in London literary society, and a member of the Bloomsbury group. Her best-known works include *Mrs. Dalloway* and *A Room of One's Own*.

Anzia Yezierska (1885–1970) emigrated with her family from Plinsk to New York City when she was fifteen. She followed her first novel, *Salome of the Tenements*, with three more novels about the Jewish immigrant experience. During the Depression, she was hired by the Works Progress Administration's Writers' Project to catalog the trees in Central Park.

The selection "Making Drudgery Divine" from "The Mistress of the House," written "By the Author of 'Isa Graeme's Word,' Etc.," was published by Hodder & Stoughton in 1894.

Global Spiritual Perspectives

Spiritual Perspectives on America's Role as Superpower
by the Editors at SkyLight Paths

Are we the world's good neighbor or a global bully? From a spiritual perspective, what are America's responsibilities as the only remaining superpower? Contributors:

Dr. Beatrice Bruteau • Dr. Joan Brown Campbell • Tony Campolo • Rev. Forrest Church • Lama Surya Das • Matthew Fox • Kabir Helminski • Thich Nhat Hanh • Eboo Patel • Abbot M. Basil Pennington, ocso • Dennis Prager • Rosemary Radford Ruether • Wayne Teasdale • Rev. William McD. Tully • Rabbi Arthur Waskow • John Wilson

5½ x 8½, 256 pp, Quality PB, 978-1-893361-81-2 **$16.95**

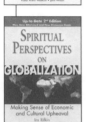

Spiritual Perspectives on Globalization, 2nd Edition
Making Sense of Economic and Cultural Upheaval
by Ira Rifkin; Foreword by Dr. David Little, Harvard Divinity School

What is globalization? Surveys the religious landscape. Includes a new Discussion Guide designed for group use.

5½ x 8½, 256 pp, Quality PB, 978-1-59473-045-0 **$16.99**

Hinduism / Vedanta

The Four Yogas
A Guide to the Spiritual Paths of Action, Devotion, Meditation and Knowledge
 by Swami Adiswarananda 6 x 9, 320 pp, HC, 978-1-59473-143-3 **$29.99**

Meditation & Its Practices
A Definitive Guide to Techniques and Traditions of Meditation in Yoga and Vedanta
 by Swami Adiswarananda 6 x 9, 504 pp, Quality PB, 978-1-59473-105-1 **$19.99**

The Spiritual Quest and the Way of Yoga: The Goal, the Journey and the Milestones
 by Swami Adiswarananda 6 x 9, 288 pp, HC, 978-1-59473-113-6 **$29.99**

Sri Ramakrishna, the Face of Silence
 by Swami Nikhilananda and Dhan Gopal Mukerji
 Edited with an Introduction by Swami Adiswarananda; Foreword by Dhan Gopal Mukerji II

Classic biographies present the life and thought of Sri Ramakrishna.
6 x 9, 352 pp, HC, 978-1-59473-115-0 **$29.99**

Sri Sarada Devi, The Holy Mother
Her Teachings and Conversations
 Translated with Notes by Swami Nikhilananda; Edited with an Introduction by Swami Adiswarananda
6 x 9, 288 pp, HC, 978-1-59473-070-2 **$29.99**

The Vedanta Way to Peace and Happiness by Swami Adiswarananda
6 x 9, 240 pp, HC, 978-1-59473-034-4 **$29.99**

Vivekananda, World Teacher: His Teachings on the Spiritual Unity of Humankind
 Edited and with an Introduction by Swami Adiswarananda
6 x 9, 272 pp, Quality PB, 978-1-59473-210-2 **$21.99**

Sikhism

The First Sikh Spiritual Master
Timeless Wisdom from the Life and Teachings of Guru Nanak by Harish Dhillon

Tells the story of a unique spiritual leader who showed a gentle, peaceful path to God-realization while highlighting Guru Nanak's quest for tolerance and compassion. 6 x 9, 192 pp, Quality PB, 978-1-59473-209-6 **$16.99**

Or phone, fax, mail or e-mail to: SKYLIGHT PATHS Publishing
Sunset Farm Offices, Route 4 • P.O. Box 237 • Woodstock, Vermont 05091
Tel: (802) 457-4000 • Fax: (802) 457-4004 • www.skylightpaths.com
Credit card orders: (800) 962-4544 (8:30AM–5:30PM ET Monday–Friday)
Generous discounts on quantity orders. SATISFACTION GUARANTEED. Prices subject to change.

Children's Spiritual Biography

Ten Amazing People
And How They Changed the World

For ages 7 & up

by Maura D. Shaw; Foreword by Dr. Robert Coles
Full-color illus. by Stephen Marchesi

Black Elk • Dorothy Day • Malcolm X • Mahatma Gandhi • Martin Luther King, Jr. • Mother Teresa • Janusz Korczak • Desmond Tutu • Thich Nhat Hanh • Albert Schweitzer

This vivid, inspirational and authoritative book will open new possibilities for children by telling the stories of how ten of the past century's greatest leaders changed the world in important ways.
8½ x 11, 48 pp, HC, Full-color illus., 978-1-893361-47-8 **$17.95**
For ages 7 & up

Spiritual Biographies for Young People—For ages 7 and up

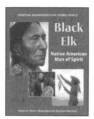 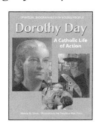 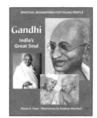 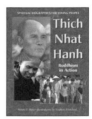

Black Elk: Native American Man of Spirit
by Maura D. Shaw; Full-color illus. by Stephen Marchesi
Through historically accurate illustrations and photos, inspiring age-appropriate activities and Black Elk's own words, this colorful biography introduces children to a remarkable person who ensured that the traditions and beliefs of his people would not be forgotten.
6¾ x 8¾, 32 pp, HC, Full-color and b/w illus., 978-1-59473-043-6 **$12.99**

Dorothy Day: A Catholic Life of Action
by Maura D. Shaw; Full-color illus. by Stephen Marchesi
Introduces children to one of the most inspiring women of the twentieth century, a down-to-earth spiritual leader who saw the presence of God in every person she met. Includes practical activities, a timeline and a list of important words to know.
6¾ x 8¾, 32 pp, HC, Full-color illus., 978-1-59473-011-5 **$12.99**

Gandhi: India's Great Soul
by Maura D. Shaw; Full-color illus. by Stephen Marchesi
There are a number of biographies of Gandhi written for young readers, but this is the only one that balances a simple text with illustrations, photographs, and activities that encourage children and adults to talk about how to make changes happen without violence. Introduces children to important concepts of freedom, equality and justice among people of all backgrounds and religions.
6¾ x 8¾, 32 pp, HC, Full-color illus., 978-1-893361-91-1 **$12.95**

Thich Nhat Hanh: Buddhism in Action
by Maura D. Shaw; Full-color illus. by Stephen Marchesi
Warm illustrations, photos, age-appropriate activities and Thich Nhat Hanh's own poems introduce a great man to children in a way they can understand and enjoy. Includes a list of important Buddhist words to know.
6¾ x 8¾, 32 pp, HC, Full-color illus., 978-1-893361-87-4 **$12.95**

Kabbalah from Jewish Lights Publishing

Awakening to Kabbalah: The Guiding Light of Spiritual Fulfillment
by Rav Michael Laitman, PhD 6 x 9, 192 pp, HC, 978-1-58023-264-7 **$21.99**

Cast in God's Image: Discover Your Personality Type Using the Enneagram and Kabbalah
by Rabbi Howard A. Addison 7 x 9, 176 pp, Quality PB, 978-1-58023-124-4 **$16.95**

Ehyeh: A Kabbalah for Tomorrow *by Dr. Arthur Green*
6 x 9, 224 pp, Quality PB, 978-1-58023-213-5 **$16.99**

The Enneagram and Kabbalah, 2nd Edition: Reading Your Soul
by Rabbi Howard A. Addison 6 x 9, 192 pp, Quality PB, 978-1-58023-229-6 **$16.99**

Finding Joy: A Practical Spiritual Guide to Happiness *by Dannel I. Schwartz with Mark Hass*
6 x 9, 192 pp, Quality PB, 978-1-58023-009-4 **$14.95**

The Gift of Kabbalah: Discovering the Secrets of Heaven, Renewing Your Life on Earth
by Tamar Frankiel, PhD 6 x 9, 256 pp, Quality PB, 978-1-58023-141-1 **$16.95**
HC, 978-1-58023-108-4 **$21.95**

Honey from the Rock: An Easy Introduction to Jewish Mysticism
by Lawrence Kushner 6 x 9, 176 pp, Quality PB, 978-1-58023-073-5 **$16.95**

Kabbalah: A Brief Introduction for Christians
by Tamar Frankiel, PhD 5½ x 8½, 176 pp, Quality PB, 978-1-58023-303-3 **$16.99**

Zohar: Annotated & Explained *Translation and Annotation by Dr. Daniel C. Matt*
Foreword by Andrew Harvey 5½ x 8½, 176 pp, Quality PB, 978-1-893361-51-5 **$15.99**

Judaism / Christianity

Christians and Jews in Dialogue: Learning in the Presence of the Other
by Mary C. Boys and Sara S. Lee; Foreword by Dorothy C. Bass
Inspires renewed commitment to dialogue between religious traditions and illuminates how it should happen. Explains the transformative work of creating environments for Jews and Christians to study together and enter the dynamism of the other's religious tradition.
6 x 9, 240 pp, HC, 978-1-59473-144-0 **$21.99**

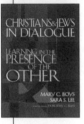

Healing the Jewish-Christian Rift: Growing Beyond Our Wounded History
by Ron Miller and Laura Bernstein; Foreword by Dr. Beatrice Bruteau
6 x 9, 288 pp, Quality PB, 978-1-59473-139-6 **$18.99**

Introducing My Faith and My Community
The Jewish Outreach Institute Guide for the Christian in a Jewish Interfaith Relationship
by Rabbi Kerry M. Olitzky 6 x 9, 176 pp, Quality PB, 978-1-58023-192-3 **$16.99** *(a Jewish Lights book)*

The Jewish Approach to God: A Brief Introduction for Christians
by Rabbi Neil Gillman 5½ x 8½, 192 pp, Quality PB, 978-1-58023-190-9 **$16.95** *(a Jewish Lights book)*

Jewish Holidays: A Brief Introduction for Christians
by Rabbi Kerry M. Olitzky and Rabbi Daniel Judson
5½ x 8½, 176 pp, Quality PB, 978-1-58023-302-6 **$16.99** *(a Jewish Lights book)*

Jewish Ritual: A Brief Introduction for Christians
by Rabbi Kerry M. Olitzky and Rabbi Daniel Judson
5½ x 8½, 144 pp, Quality PB, 978-1-58023-210-4 **$14.99** *(a Jewish Lights book)*

Jewish Spirituality: A Brief Introduction for Christians
by Rabbi Lawrence Kushner
5½ x 8½, 112 pp, Quality PB, 978-1-58023-150-3 **$12.95** *(a Jewish Lights book)*

A Jewish Understanding of the New Testament
by Rabbi Samuel Sandmel; new Preface by Rabbi David Sandmel
5½ x 8½, 368 pp, Quality PB, 978-1-59473-048-1 **$19.99**

We Jews and Jesus
Exploring Theological Differences for Mutual Understanding
by Rabbi Samuel Sandmel; new Preface by Rabbi David Sandmel A Classic Reprint
Written in a non-technical way for the layperson, this candid and forthright look at the what and why of the Jewish attitude toward Jesus is a clear and forceful exposition that guides both Christians and Jews in relevant discussion.
6 x 9, 192 pp, Quality PB, 978-1-59473-208-9 **$16.99**

Midrash Fiction / Folktales

Abraham's Bind & Other Bible Tales of Trickery, Folly, Mercy and Love *by Michael J. Caduto*

New retellings of episodes in the lives of familiar biblical characters explore relevant life lessons.

6 x 9, 224 pp, HC, 978-1-59473-186-0 **$19.99**

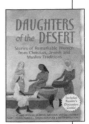

Daughters of the Desert: Stories of Remarkable Women from Christian, Jewish and Muslim Traditions *by Claire Rudolf Murphy, Meghan Nuttall Sayres, Mary Cronk Farrell, Sarah Conover and Betsy Wharton*

Breathes new life into the old tales of our female ancestors in faith. Uses traditional scriptural passages as starting points, then with vivid detail fills in historical context and place. Chapters reveal the voices of Sarah, Hagar, Huldah, Esther, Salome, Mary Magdalene, Lydia, Khadija, Fatima and many more. Historical fiction ideal for readers of all ages. Quality paperback includes reader's discussion guide.

5½ x 8½, 192 pp, Quality PB, 978-1-59473-106-8 **$14.99**
HC, 192 pp, 978-1-893361-72-0 **$19.95**

The Triumph of Eve & Other Subversive Bible Tales
by Matt Biers-Ariel

Many people were taught and remember only a one-dimensional Bible. These engaging retellings are the antidote to this—they're witty, often hilarious, always profound, and invite you to grapple with questions and issues that are often hidden in the original text.

5½ x 8½, 192 pp, Quality PB, 978-1-59473-176-1 **$14.99**
HC, 192 pp, 978-1-59473-040-5 **$19.99**

Also avail.: **The Triumph of Eve Teacher's Guide**
8½ x 11, 44 pp, PB, 978-1-59473-152-5 **$8.99**

Wisdom in the Telling
Finding Inspiration and Grace in Traditional Folktales and Myths Retold
by Lorraine Hartin-Gelardi
6 x 9, 224 pp, HC, 978-1-59473-185-3 **$19.99**

Religious Etiquette / Reference

How to Be a Perfect Stranger, 4th Edition: The Essential Religious Etiquette Handbook *Edited by Stuart M. Matlins and Arthur J. Magida*

The indispensable guidebook to help the well-meaning guest when visiting other people's religious ceremonies. A straightforward guide to the rituals and celebrations of the major religions and denominations in the United States and Canada from the perspective of an interested guest of any other faith, based on information obtained from authorities of each religion. Belongs in every living room, library and office. Covers:

African American Methodist Churches • Assemblies of God • Bahá'í • Baptist • Buddhist • Christian Church (Disciples of Christ) • Christian Science (Church of Christ, Scientist) • Churches of Christ • Episcopalian and Anglican • Hindu • Islam • Jehovah's Witnesses • Jewish • Lutheran • Mennonite/Amish • Methodist • Mormon (Church of Jesus Christ of Latter-day Saints) • Native American/First Nations • Orthodox Churches • Pentecostal Church of God • Presbyterian • Quaker (Religious Society of Friends) • Reformed Church in America/Canada • Roman Catholic • Seventh-day Adventist • Sikh • Unitarian Universalist • United Church of Canada • United Church of Christ

6 x 9, 432 pp, Quality PB, 978-1-59473-140-2 **$19.99**

The Perfect Stranger's Guide to Funerals and Grieving Practices: A Guide to Etiquette in Other People's Religious Ceremonies *Edited by Stuart M. Matlins*
6 x 9, 240 pp, Quality PB, 978-1-893361-20-1 **$16.95**

The Perfect Stranger's Guide to Wedding Ceremonies: A Guide to Etiquette in Other People's Religious Ceremonies *Edited by Stuart M. Matlins*
6 x 9, 208 pp, Quality PB, 978-1-893361-19-5 **$16.95**

Sacred Texts—SkyLight Illuminations Series

Offers today's spiritual seeker an accessible entry into the great classic texts of the world's spiritual traditions. Each classic is presented in an accessible translation, with facing pages of guided commentary from experts, giving you the keys you need to understand the history, context and meaning of the text. This series enables you, whatever your background, to experience and understand classic spiritual texts directly, and to make them a part of your life.

CHRISTIANITY

The End of Days: Essential Selections from Apocalyptic Texts—
Annotated & Explained   *Annotation by Robert G. Clouse*
Helps you understand the complex Christian visions of the end of the world.
5½ x 8½, 224 pp, Quality PB, 978-1-59473-170-9 **$16.99**

The Hidden Gospel of Matthew: Annotated & Explained
Translation & Annotation by Ron Miller
Takes you deep into the text cherished around the world to discover the words and events that have the strongest connection to the historical Jesus.
5½ x 8½, 272 pp, Quality PB, 978-1-59473-038-2 **$16.99**

The Lost Sayings of Jesus: Teachings from Ancient Christian, Jewish, Gnostic and Islamic Sources—Annotated & Explained
Translation & Annotation by Andrew Phillip Smith; Foreword by Stephan A. Hoeller
This collection of more than three hundred sayings depicts Jesus as a Wisdom teacher who speaks to people of all faiths as a mystic and spiritual master.
5½ x 8½, 240 pp, Quality PB, 978-1-59473-172-3 **$16.99**

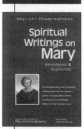

Philokalia: The Eastern Christian Spiritual Texts—Selections Annotated & Explained   *Annotation by Allyne Smith; Translation by G. E. H. Palmer, Phillip Sherrard and Bishop Kallistos Ware*
The first approachable introduction to the wisdom of the Philokalia, which is the classic text of Eastern Christian spirituality.
5½ x 8½, 240 pp, Quality PB, 978-1-59473-103-7 **$16.99**

Spiritual Writings on Mary: Annotated & Explained
Annotation by Mary Ford-Grabowsky; Foreword by Andrew Harvey
Examines the role of Mary, the mother of Jesus, as a source of inspiration in history and in life today.   5½ x 8½, 288 pp, Quality PB, 978-1-59473-001-6 **$16.99**

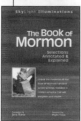

The Way of a Pilgrim: Annotated & Explained
Translation & Annotation by Gleb Pokrovsky; Foreword by Andrew Harvey
This classic of Russian spirituality is the delightful account of one man who sets out to learn the prayer of the heart, also known as the "Jesus prayer."
5½ x 8½, 160 pp, Illus., Quality PB, 978-1-893361-31-7 **$14.95**

MORMONISM

The Book of Mormon: Selections Annotated & Explained
Annotation by Jana Riess; Foreword by Phyllis Tickle
Explores the sacred epic that is cherished by more than twelve million members of the LDS church as the keystone of their faith.
5½ x 8½ , 272 pp, Quality PB, 978-1-59473-076-4 **$16.99**

NATIVE AMERICAN

Native American Stories of the Sacred: Annotated & Explained
Retold & Annotated by Evan T. Pritchard
Intended for more than entertainment, these teaching tales contain elegantly simple illustrations of time-honored truths.
5½ x 8½, 272 pp, Quality PB, 978-1-59473-112-9 **$16.99**

Sacred Texts—cont.

GNOSTICISM

The Gospel of Philip: Annotated & Explained
Translation & Annotation by Andrew Phillip Smith; Foreword by Stevan Davies
Reveals otherwise unrecorded sayings of Jesus and fragments of Gnostic mythology.
5½ x 8½, 160 pp, Quality PB, 978-1-59473-111-2 **$16.99**

The Gospel of Thomas: Annotated & Explained
Translation & Annotation by Stevan Davies Sheds new light on the origins of Christianity and
portrays Jesus as a wisdom-loving sage. 5½ x 8½, 192 pp, Quality PB, 978-1-893361-45-4 **$16.99**

The Secret Book of John: The Gnostic Gospel—Annotated & Explained
Translation & Annotation by Stevan Davies The most significant and influential text of
the ancient Gnostic religion. 5½ x 8½, 208 pp, Quality PB, 978-1-59473-082-5 **$16.99**

JUDAISM

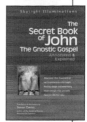

The Divine Feminine in Biblical Wisdom Literature
Selections Annotated & Explained
Translation & Annotation by Rabbi Rami Shapiro; Foreword by Rev. Cynthia Bourgeault, PhD
Uses the Hebrew books of Psalms, Proverbs, Song of Songs, Ecclesiastes and Job,
Wisdom literature and the Wisdom of Solomon to clarify who Wisdom is.
5½ x 8½, 240 pp, Quality PB, 978-1-59473-109-9 **$16.99**

Ethics of the Sages: *Pirke Avot*—Annotated & Explained
Translation & Annotation by Rabbi Rami Shapiro Clarifies the ethical teachings of the
early Rabbis. 5½ x 8½, 192 pp, Quality PB, 978-1-59473-207-2 **$16.99**

Hasidic Tales: Annotated & Explained
Translation & Annotation by Rabbi Rami Shapiro
Introduces the legendary tales of the impassioned Hasidic rabbis, presenting them as
stories rather than as parables. 5½ x 8½, 240 pp, Quality PB, 978-1-893361-86-7 **$16.95**

The Hebrew Prophets: Selections Annotated & Explained
Translation & Annotation by Rabbi Rami Shapiro; Foreword by Zalman M. Schachter-Shalomi
Focuses on the central themes covered by all the Hebrew prophets.
5½ x 8½, 224 pp, Quality PB, 978-1-59473-037-5 **$16.99**

Zohar: Annotated & Explained *Translation & Annotation by Daniel C. Matt*
The best-selling author of *The Essential Kabbalah* brings together in one place the most
important teachings of the Zohar, the canonical text of Jewish mystical tradition.
5½ x 8½, 176 pp, Quality PB, 978-1-893361-51-5 **$15.99**

EASTERN RELIGIONS

Bhagavad Gita: Annotated & Explained *Translation by Shri Purohit Swami*
Annotation by Kendra Crossen Burroughs Explains references and philosophical terms,
shares the interpretations of famous spiritual leaders and scholars, and more.
5½ x 8½, 192 pp, Quality PB, 978-1-893361-28-7 **$16.95**

Dhammapada: Annotated & Explained *Translation by Max Müller and revised by*
Jack Maguire; Annotation by Jack Maguire Contains all of Buddhism's key teachings.
5½ x 8½, 160 pp, b/w photos, Quality PB, 978-1-893361-42-3 **$14.95**

Rumi and Islam: Selections from His Stories, Poems, and Discourses—
Annotated & Explained *Translation & Annotation by Ibrahim Gamard*
Focuses on Rumi's place within the Sufi tradition of Islam, providing insight into
the mystical side of the religion. 5½ x 8½, 240 pp, Quality PB, 978-1-59473-002-3 **$15.99**

Selections from the Gospel of Sri Ramakrishna: Annotated & Explained
Translation by Swami Nikhilananda; Annotation by Kendra Crossen Burroughs
Introduces the fascinating world of the Indian mystic and the universal appeal
of his message. 5½ x 8½, 240 pp, b/w photos, Quality PB, 978-1-893361-46-1 **$16.95**

Tao Te Ching: Annotated & Explained *Translation & Annotation by Derek Lin*
Foreword by Lama Surya Das Introduces an Eastern classic in an accessible, poetic
and completely original way. 5½ x 8½, 192 pp, Quality PB, 978-1-59473-204-1 **$16.99**

Spiritual Poetry—The Mystic Poets

Experience these mystic poets as you never have before. Each beautiful, compact book includes: a brief introduction to the poet's time and place; a summary of the major themes of the poet's mysticism and religious tradition; essential selections from the poet's most important works; and an appreciative preface by a contemporary spiritual writer.

   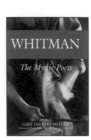

Hafiz: The Mystic Poets
Preface by Ibrahim Gamard
Hafiz is known throughout the world as Persia's greatest poet, with sales of his poems in Iran today only surpassed by those of the Qur'an itself. His probing and joyful verse speaks to people from all backgrounds who long to taste and feel divine love and experience harmony with all living things.
5 x 7¼, 144 pp, HC, 978-1-59473-009-2 **$16.99**

Hopkins: The Mystic Poets
Preface by Rev. Thomas Ryan, CSP
Gerard Manley Hopkins, Christian mystical poet, is beloved for his use of fresh language and startling metaphors to describe the world around him. Although his verse is lovely, beneath the surface lies a searching soul, wrestling with and yearning for God.
5 x 7¼, 112 pp, HC, 978-1-59473-010-8 **$16.99**

Tagore: The Mystic Poets
Preface by Swami Adiswarananda
Rabindranath Tagore is often considered the "Shakespeare" of modern India. A great mystic, Tagore was the teacher of W. B. Yeats and Robert Frost, the close friend of Albert Einstein and Mahatma Gandhi, and the winner of the Nobel Prize for Literature. This beautiful sampling of Tagore's two most important works, *The Gardener* and *Gitanjali,* offers a glimpse into his spiritual vision that has inspired people around the world.
5 x 7¼, 144 pp, HC, 978-1-59473-008-5 **$16.99**

Whitman: The Mystic Poets
Preface by Gary David Comstock
Walt Whitman was the most innovative and influential poet of the nineteenth century. This beautiful sampling of Whitman's most important poetry from *Leaves of Grass,* and selections from his prose writings, offers a glimpse into the spiritual side of his most radical themes—love for country, love for others, and love of Self.
5 x 7¼, 192 pp, HC, 978-1-59473-041-2 **$16.99**

Spiritual Biography—SkyLight Lives

SkyLight Lives reintroduces the lives and works of key spiritual figures of our time—people who by their teaching or example have challenged our assumptions about spirituality and have caused us to look at it in new ways.

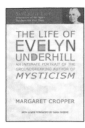 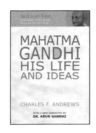 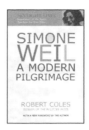 

The Life of Evelyn Underhill
An Intimate Portrait of the Groundbreaking Author of *Mysticism*
by Margaret Cropper; Foreword by Dana Greene
Evelyn Underhill was a passionate writer and teacher who wrote elegantly on mysticism, worship, and devotional life.
6 x 9, 288 pp, 5 b/w photos, Quality PB, 978-1-893361-70-6 **$18.95**

Mahatma Gandhi: His Life and Ideas
by Charles F. Andrews; Foreword by Dr. Arun Gandhi
Examines from a contemporary Christian activist's point of view the religious ideas and political dynamics that influenced the birth of the peaceful resistance movement.
6 x 9, 336 pp, 5 b/w photos, Quality PB, 978-1-893361-89-8 **$18.95**

Simone Weil: A Modern Pilgrimage
by Robert Coles
The extraordinary life of the spiritual philosopher who's been called both saint and madwoman.
6 x 9, 208 pp, Quality PB, 978-1-893361-34-8 **$16.95**

Zen Effects: The Life of Alan Watts
by Monica Furlong
Through his widely popular books and lectures, Alan Watts (1915–1973) did more to introduce Eastern philosophy and religion to Western minds than any figure before or since.
6 x 9, 264 pp, Quality PB, 978-1-893361-32-4 **$16.95**

More Spiritual Biography

Bede Griffiths: An Introduction to His Interspiritual Thought
by Wayne Teasdale
The first study of his contemplative experience and thought, exploring the intersection of Hinduism and Christianity.
6 x 9, 288 pp, Quality PB, 978-1-893361-77-5 **$18.95**

The Soul of the Story: Meetings with Remarkable People
by Rabbi David Zeller
Inspiring and entertaining, this compelling collection of spiritual adventures assures us that no spiritual lesson truly learned is ever lost.
6 x 9, 288 pp, HC, 978-1-58023-272-2 **$21.99** *(a Jewish Lights book)*

Spirituality

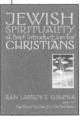

Jewish Spirituality: A Brief Introduction for Christians   *by Lawrence Kushner*
5½ x 8½, 112 pp, Quality PB, 978-1-58023-150-3 **$12.95** *(a Jewish Lights book)*

Journeys of Simplicity: Traveling Light with Thomas Merton, Bashō, Edward Abbey, Annie Dillard & Others *by Philip Harnden* 5 x 7¼, 128 pp, HC, 978-1-893361-76-8 **$16.95**

Keeping Spiritual Balance As We Grow Older: More than 65 Creative Ways to Use Purpose, Prayer, and the Power of Spirit to Build a Meaningful Retirement *by Molly and Bernie Srode* 8 x 8, 224 pp, Quality PB, 978-1-59473-042-9 **$16.99**

The Monks of Mount Athos: A Western Monk's Extraordinary Spiritual Journey on Eastern Holy Ground *by M. Basil Pennington, ocso; Foreword by Archimandrite Dionysios* 6 x 9, 256 pp, 10+ b/w line drawings, Quality PB, 978-1-893361-78-2 **$18.95**

One God Clapping: The Spiritual Path of a Zen Rabbi *by Alan Lew with Sherrill Jaffe* 5½ x 8½, 336 pp, Quality PB, 978-1-58023-115-2 **$16.95** *(a Jewish Lights book)*

Prayer for People Who Think Too Much: A Guide to Everyday, Anywhere Prayer from the World's Faith Traditions *by Mitch Finley* 5½ x 8½, 224 pp, Quality PB, 978-1-893361-21-8 **$16.99**; HC, 978-1-893361-00-3 **$21.95**

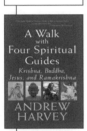

Show Me Your Way: The Complete Guide to Exploring Interfaith Spiritual Direction *by Howard A. Addison* 5½ x 8½, 240 pp, Quality PB, 978-1-893361-41-6 **$16.95**

Spirituality 101: The Indispensable Guide to Keeping—or Finding—Your Spiritual Life on Campus *by Harriet L. Schwartz, with contributions from college students at nearly thirty campuses across the United States* 6 x 9, 272 pp, Quality PB, 978-1-59473-000-9 **$16.99**

Spiritually Incorrect: Finding God in All the *Wrong* Places *by Dan Wakefield; Illus. by Marian DelVecchio* 5½ x 8½, 192 pp, b/w illus., Quality PB, 978-1-59473-137-2 **$15.99**

Spiritual Manifestos: Visions for Renewed Religious Life in America from Young Spiritual Leaders of Many Faiths *Edited by Niles Elliot Goldstein; Preface by Martin E. Marty* 6 x 9, 256 pp, HC, 978-1-893361-09-6 **$21.95**

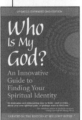

A Walk with Four Spiritual Guides: Krishna, Buddha, Jesus, and Ramakrishna *by Andrew Harvey* 5½ x 8½, 192 pp, 10 b/w photos & illus., Quality PB, 978-1-59473-138-9 **$15.99**

What Matters: Spiritual Nourishment for Head and Heart *by Frederick Franck* 5 x 7¼, 128 pp, 50+ b/w illus., HC, 978-1-59473-013-9 **$16.99**

Who Is My God?, 2nd Edition: An Innovative Guide to Finding Your Spiritual Identity *Created by the Editors at SkyLight Paths* 6 x 9, 160 pp, Quality PB, 978-1-59473-014-6 **$15.99**

Spirituality—A Week Inside

Come and Sit: A Week Inside Meditation Centers
by Marcia Z. Nelson; Foreword by Wayne Teasdale
The insider's guide to meditation in a variety of different spiritual traditions—Buddhist, Hindu, Christian, Jewish, and Sufi traditions.
6 x 9, 224 pp, b/w photos, Quality PB, 978-1-893361-35-5 **$16.95**

Lighting the Lamp of Wisdom: A Week Inside a Yoga Ashram
by John Ittner; Foreword by Dr. David Frawley
This insider's guide to Hindu spiritual life takes you into a typical week of retreat inside a yoga ashram to demystify the experience and show you what to expect.
6 x 9, 192 pp, 10+ b/w photos, Quality PB, 978-1-893361-52-2 **$15.95**

Making a Heart for God: A Week Inside a Catholic Monastery
by Dianne Aprile; Foreword by Brother Patrick Hart, ocso
Takes you to the Abbey of Gethsemani—the Trappist monastery in Kentucky that was home to author Thomas Merton—to explore the details.
6 x 9, 224 pp, b/w photos, Quality PB, 978-1-893361-49-2 **$16.95**

Waking Up: A Week Inside a Zen Monastery
by Jack Maguire; Foreword by John Daido Loori, Roshi
An essential guide to what it's like to spend a week inside a Zen Buddhist monastery.
6 x 9, 224 pp, b/w photos, Quality PB, 978-1-893361-55-3 **$16.95**
HC, 978-1-893361-13-3 **$21.95**

Spirituality of the Seasons

Autumn: A Spiritual Biography of the Season
Edited by Gary Schmidt and Susan M. Felch; Illustrations by Mary Azarian
Rejoice in autumn as a time of preparation and reflection. Includes Wendell Berry, David James Duncan, Robert Frost, A. Bartlett Giamatti, E. B. White, P. D. James, Julian of Norwich, Garret Keizer, Tracy Kidder, Anne Lamott, May Sarton.
6 x 9, 320 pp, 5 b/w illus., Quality PB, 978-1-59473-118-1 **$18.99**
HC, 978-1-59473-005-4 **$22.99**

Spring: A Spiritual Biography of the Season
Edited by Gary Schmidt and Susan M. Felch; Illustrations by Mary Azarian
Explore the gentle unfurling of spring and reflect on how nature celebrates rebirth and renewal. Includes Jane Kenyon, Lucy Larcom, Harry Thurston, Nathaniel Hawthorne, Noel Perrin, Annie Dillard, Martha Ballard, Barbara Kingsolver, Dorothy Wordsworth, Donald Hall, David Brill, Lionel Basney, Isak Dinesen, Paul Laurence Dunbar.
6 x 9, 352 pp, 6 b/w illus., HC, 978-1-59473-114-3 **$21.99**

Summer: A Spiritual Biography of the Season
Edited by Gary Schmidt and Susan M. Felch; Illustrations by Barry Moser
"A sumptuous banquet.... These selections lift up an exquisite wholeness found within an everyday sophistication."— ★ *Publishers Weekly* starred review
Includes Anne Lamott, Luci Shaw, Ray Bradbury, Richard Selzer, Thomas Lynch, Walt Whitman, Carl Sandburg, Sherman Alexie, Madeleine L'Engle, Jamaica Kincaid.
6 x 9, 304 pp, 5 b/w illus., HC, 978-1-59473-083-2 **$21.99**

Winter: A Spiritual Biography of the Season
Edited by Gary Schmidt and Susan M. Felch; Illustrations by Barry Moser
"This outstanding anthology features top-flight nature and spirituality writers on the fierce, inexorable season of winter.... Remarkably lively and warm, despite the icy subject." — ★ *Publishers Weekly* starred review.
Includes Will Campbell, Rachel Carson, Annie Dillard, Donald Hall, Ron Hansen, Jane Kenyon, Jamaica Kincaid, Barry Lopez, Kathleen Norris, John Updike, E. B. White.
6 x 9, 288 pp, 6 b/w illus., Deluxe PB w/flaps, 978-1-893361-92-8 **$18.95**
HC, 978-1-893361-53-9 **$21.95**

Spirituality / Animal Companions

Blessing the Animals: Prayers and Ceremonies to Celebrate God's Creatures, Wild and Tame   *Edited by Lynn L. Caruso* 5 x 7¼, 256 pp, HC, 978-1-59473-145-7 **$19.99**

What Animals Can Teach Us about Spirituality: Inspiring Lessons from Wild and Tame Creatures *by Diana L. Guerrero* 6 x 9, 176 pp, Quality PB, 978-1-893361-84-3 **$16.95**

Spirituality

Awakening the Spirit, Inspiring the Soul
30 Stories of Interspiritual Discovery in the Community of Faiths
Edited by Brother Wayne Teasdale and Martha Howard, MD; Foreword by Joan Borysenko, PhD
Thirty original spiritual mini-autobiographies showcase the varied ways that people come to faith—and what that means—in today's multi-religious world.
6 x 9, 224 pp, HC, 978-1-59473-039-9 **$21.99**

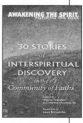

The Alphabet of Paradise: An A–Z of Spirituality for Everyday Life
 by Howard Cooper 5 x 7¾, 224 pp, Quality PB, 978-1-893361-80-5 **$16.95**

Creating a Spiritual Retirement: A Guide to the Unseen Possibilities in Our Lives
 by Molly Srode 6 x 9, 208 pp, b/w photos, Quality PB, 978-1-59473-050-4 **$14.99**
HC, 978-1-893361-75-1 **$19.95**

Finding Hope: Cultivating God's Gift of a Hopeful Spirit
 by Marcia Ford 8 x 8, 200 pp, Quality PB, 978-1-59473-211-9 **$16.99**

The Geography of Faith: Underground Conversations on Religious, Political and Social Change *by Daniel Berrigan and Robert Coles* 6 x 9, 224 pp, Quality PB, 978-1-893361-40-9 **$16.95**

God Within: Our Spiritual Future—As Told by Today's New Adults   *Edited by Jon M. Sweeney and the Editors at SkyLight Paths* 6 x 9, 176 pp, Quality PB, 978-1-893361-15-7 **$14.95**

Spirituality & Crafts

The Knitting Way: A Guide to Spiritual Self-Discovery
by Linda Skolnik and Janice MacDaniels
7 x 9, 240 pp, Quality PB, 978-1-59473-079-5 **$16.99**

The Quilting Path
A Guide to Spiritual Discovery through Fabric, Thread and Kabbalah
by Louise Silk
7 x 9, 192 pp, Quality PB, 978-1-59473-206-5 **$16.99**

Spiritual Practice

Divining the Body
Reclaim the Holiness of Your Physical Self *by Jan Phillips*
A practical and inspiring guidebook for connecting the body and soul in spiritual practice. Leads you into a milieu of reverence, mystery and delight, helping you discover your body as a pathway to the Divine.
8 x 8, 256 pp, Quality PB, 978-1-59473-080-1 **$16.99**

Finding Time for the Timeless: Spirituality in the Workweek
by John McQuiston II
Simple, refreshing stories that provide you with examples of how you can refocus and enrich your daily life using prayer or meditation, ritual and other forms of spiritual practice. 5½ x 6¾, 208 pp, HC, 978-1-59473-035-1 **$17.99**

The Gospel of Thomas
A Guidebook for Spiritual Practice *by Ron Miller; Translations by Stevan Davies*
An innovative guide to bring a new spiritual classic into daily life.
6 x 9, 160 pp, Quality PB, 978-1-59473-047-4 **$14.99**

Earth, Water, Fire, and Air: Essential Ways of Connecting to Spirit
by Cait Johnson 6 x 9, 224 pp, HC, 978-1-893361-65-2 **$19.95**

Labyrinths from the Outside In: Walking to Spiritual Insight—A Beginner's Guide
by Donna Schaper and Carole Ann Camp
6 x 9, 208 pp, b/w illus. and photos, Quality PB, 978-1-893361-18-8 **$16.95**

Practicing the Sacred Art of Listening: A Guide to Enrich Your Relationships
and Kindle Your Spiritual Life—The Listening Center Workshop
by Kay Lindahl 8 x 8, 176 pp, Quality PB, 978-1-893361-85-0 **$16.95**

Releasing the Creative Spirit: Unleash the Creativity in Your Life
by Dan Wakefield 7 x 10, 256 pp, Quality PB, 978-1-893361-36-2 **$16.95**

The Sacred Art of Bowing: Preparing to Practice
by Andi Young 5½ x 8½, 128 pp, b/w illus., Quality PB, 978-1-893361-82-9 **$14.95**

The Sacred Art of Chant: Preparing to Practice
by Ana Hernández 5½ x 8½, 192 pp, Quality PB, 978-1-59473-036-8 **$15.99**

The Sacred Art of Fasting: Preparing to Practice
by Thomas Ryan, CSP 5½ x 8½, 192 pp, Quality PB, 978-1-59473-078-8 **$15.99**

The Sacred Art of Forgiveness: Forgiving Ourselves and Others through God's Grace
by Marcia Ford 8 x 8, 176 pp, Quality PB, 978-1-59473-175-4 **$16.99**

The Sacred Art of Listening: Forty Reflections for Cultivating a Spiritual Practice
by Kay Lindahl; Illustrations by Amy Schnapper
8 x 8, 160 pp, b/w illus., Quality PB, 978-1-893361-44-7 **$16.99**

The Sacred Art of Lovingkindness: Preparing to Practice
by Rabbi Rami Shapiro; Foreword by Marcia Ford
5½ x 8½, 176 pp, Quality PB, 978-1-59473-151-8 **$16.99**

Sacred Speech: A Practical Guide for Keeping Spirit in Your Speech
by Rev. Donna Schaper 6 x 9, 176 pp, Quality PB, 978-1-59473-068-9 **$15.99**
HC, 978-1-893361-74-4 **$21.95**

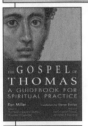